Seat of the Pants
Prayer Journey

Sarah Elizabeth Farrow

NEEDLE ROCK
PRESS

Visit Needle Rock Press at www.needlerockpress.com

Visit Sarah Elizabeth Farrow's Website at www.sarahelizabethfarrow.com

Sarah Farrow can be found on Facebook.

Praying by the Seat of Your Pants

Needle Rock Press
341 Flounce Rock Rd.
Prospect, OR 97536

Needle Rock Press books may be purchased in bulk for ministry purposes. For information, please email sandy@sandycathcartauthor.com

ISBN-10: 1-943500-16-9

ISBN-13: 978-1-943500-16-1 (Needle Rock Press)

First
to my husband John
who lived this book
with me for 53 years.

And then
to my dear friend,
Sandy Cathcart,
without whom
this book would never have happened.

My beloved speaks and says to me:
"Arise, my love, my fair one,
and come away."

—Song of Solomon 2:10 (NRSV)

About This Book

Seat of the Pants Prayer Journey is an intimate look into the prayer life of Sarah Elizabeth Farrow. Her experiences with God shared within the pages of this book really touched my life. At times I laughed, other times I cried, and throughout every story I sat in wonder of our amazing Creator.

This is the story of how Sarah learned that prayer is not a complicated thing. It's really simple and easy. You don't even have to have faith to pray. Faith comes through praying.

Sarah's story is one of discovery as she tries out all kinds of ways to get in touch with God and opens her heart to Him. To her wonder and amazement, she learns God hears prayers arising from worry. He is also the first of the first responders in emergencies. He even accepts prayers offered from some very messy altars.

Sarah's stories will lead you on your own prayer journey and show you how to navigate by the "seat of the pants," that is by experience, judgment and instinct. In the end, you will discover a more intimate relationship with your Creator than you ever thought possible.

—*Sandy Cathcart*

Note from the Author

The stories in this book are drawn from Sarah Elizabeth Farrow's own life, but in some instances names and details have been changed to protect the identity of others.

Introduction

I used to think I could teach others how to pray. I've lived longer now and know true prayer cannot be taught. Our Holy Father God meets each person in the present moment of his or her life and issues an invitation to go on a journey fraught with both danger and delight. That's why I use "seat of the pants" as a metaphor for the prayer journey.

Prayer is not something you think, say or do. Prayer is not a method or a rule. Prayer is a journey you embark on the moment you acknowledge your need of God. It takes you off the highway and onto the backroads and byways of life. And don't expect the path to be linear. Often it's more like one of those circular drives in a multi-story parking garage. You keep passing through the same point over and over, but each time you are a level higher.

Some days your path will be sunlit and smooth sailing. Others, it can be dark and scary. Expect bumps, curves and U-turns. Do not be surprised by long desert stretches, nor dismayed when you find yourself on a sidetrack or at what seems to be a dead end. The only way to get lost is to quit praying.

Prayer is indeed a journey. Yet the final destination is not a place where you arrive. Rather it is a birth—and you yourself become Prayer.

—*Sarah Elizabeth Farrow*

Contents

PART ONE: 1

Got Worry? Try Prayer

1. A Community of Faith 3
2. Growing Faith 9
3. Finding Faith 13
4. Prayer Worriers 17
5. The Cat Came Back 21
6. Green Lights all the Way 27
7. Lift up Your Hearts 33

PART TWO: 39

Got Troubles? Try Trust

8. Tornado Warning 41
9. Forgiving is Freeing 45
10. Angels Without Wings 51
11. Mothers Can't be Everywhere 57
12. Miracles do Happen 65
13. Gone in a Heartbeat 71
14. Wilderness Rescue...................... 77

PART THREE: 85

God Listens. Do We?

15. The Dog Who Wouldn't Let Me Give Up 87
16. One Baby, Two Mothers 93
17. Hearing Angels 99
18. Holy Spirit GPS 103
19. Murphy's Law 109
20. No Magic Formula 117
21. When in Doubt, Don't 121

Contents (contd.)

PART FOUR: 131
Running on Empty? Recharge
   22. God on the Mountain 133
   23. Father Knows Best 139
   24. Jesus at the Wheel 145
   25. Masada 151
   26. This is Church 157
   27. Messy Altars 161
   28. Imagine Good 167

AUTHOR CONTACT 172
AUTHOR BIO 173

Part One

Got Worry?
Try Prayer.

*We don't need faith to pray.
Faith comes through prayer.*

A Community of Faith

MY CHEEKS WERE WET WITH TEARS when I hung up the phone. After checking on my toddler, who was happily running a big plastic dump truck around the living room floor, I quickly ducked into the kitchen to collect myself.

I had just received news of a family in our car club who had been hit head-on by a drunken driver and had sustained devastating injuries. Bob hovered near death in intensive care. Jenny had sustained multiple broken bones and, after hours of surgery, was in a full-body cast. Their baby girl, barely three months old, suffered a fractured skull. She was at Children's Hospital where a shunt had been inserted to drain fluid from her swollen brain. The extent of her brain injuries were not yet known.

I desperately needed to do something, but I had no idea what. Send a card? Send flowers? Those gestures seemed woefully inadequate and somehow inappropriate. All I could think of to help was pray, but my prayers also seemed inadequate. Then I had an idea.

Recently, my husband and I had started attending church, and I knew from the pew bulletins that this congregation maintained a list of prayer needs. The list was given to the women's Wednesday morning prayer group and another group that met Friday night. The pastor also prayed for people in the Sunday morning service.

I wasn't sure they would pray for someone outside their church, but I decided to give it a shot. I checked again on Christopher, who was still happily busy with his truck, before calling the church office. The secretary answered on the second ring.

"We've been coming to church for a couple of months now," I said, "and I noticed there's a parish prayer list."

"Yes. Is there something or someone you need prayer for?"

"Well," I started, "do they have to be members?"

"Of course not." Her voice was warm and friendly. "We pray for family, friends, all sorts of people. This is a community of faith. Reaching out to others with support and prayer is what we do."

I told her about Bob, Jenny, and their precious baby. She said she had added them to the list as we talked and assured me Pastor would also remember them in the Sunday morning service.

"Did you happen to take home the Parish Directory," she asked. I told her I had. "Since this is so urgent, why don't you call some of the folks you've met and ask them to start praying now."

"But…" I stammered, "I don't know anyone very well yet." I couldn't believe she was telling me to call strangers.

"Don't worry about it," she said. "Just call. Sharing prayer needs is a great way to get to know others."

By the time our conversation ended, Christopher had grown tired of his truck and was getting fussy, so I gave him a snack and we cuddled in the rocking chair for a bit. My tears started to flow again as I held my much-loved little guy. I couldn't even imagine the pain of lying immobilized in a hospital bed knowing my baby was in another hospital miles away with a fractured skull.

"Holy Father God," I murmured, "be with Bob and Jenny in this time of trial. Take care of their baby."

When Christopher drifted off, I tucked him into his crib for a nap. Then I pulled out the Parish Directory and started looking for names I recognized. One jumped out right away. Sue had sat next to me a week ago. Her boy was the same age as Christopher, and she had suggested we get together for a play date. I called her.

"Hi," I started, "I'm not sure you remember me, but we sat together in the adult Sunday school last week."

"Oh, I'm so glad you called! I forgot to get your number, and I wanted to set up that play date we talked about."

I quickly explained that wasn't the reason for my call. Then I told her what had happened to our car club friends. "Would you mind praying for them?" I asked.

"Of course, I'll pray for them," She said.

Her immediate willingness surprised me. I didn't realize people prayed for others they didn't even know.

"Even better," Sue said, "I'll set up a prayer chain for Bob, Jenny, and their baby."

"What's that?" I asked.

She patiently explained she would call other women in the parish, give them the information, and they would join us in prayer as the Holy Spirit led. Then she asked if I remembered the story in the Bible where some men brought their friend to a home where Jesus was teaching and lowered him through the roof so Jesus could heal him.

"I do," I said.

"That's what we are doing for these folks. We are all working together to lift them up to Jesus so he can heal them."

As Sue requested, I was careful to provide updates as our friends' healing progressed. The road to recovery for Bob, Jenny, and their baby was a long one. It was touch-and-go at first for Bob whose aorta had been damaged and came dangerously close to tearing. Jenny spent several weeks in rehab before she was able to go home. Wonderfully, baby Anna healed better than her doctors expected and showed no signs of brain damage.

In time, we were able to pray in thanksgiving for the healing of this family. By then I had gotten to know not only Sue, but all the women in her prayer chain and thought of them as good friends. I was amazed at how faithful they all had been to join me in prayer even though they didn't know Bob, Jenny, and their baby and probably never would. When I mentioned this to Sue, she just smiled and said, "Prayer is the work of a community of faith. It's simply what we do."

Since that time, I've often called upon my community of faith to join me in prayer for many different things. It's nice to know others are coming alongside me and adding their faith to mine, especially whenever I'm too involved emotionally or too exhausted to pray as often as I would like. With a community of prayer warriors, someone is always lifting our requests up to Holy Father God.

Thank You Note

Thank you, Holy Father God,
for gathering many hearts together
and making them into a community of faith.
Thank you for their willingness to pray for my friends
even when they didn't know them.
Thank you for all the ways
this community is your hands,
your feet and your voice in the world.

Growing
Faith

I WAS ENJOYING COFFEE WITH FRIENDS.

"I attended the Joyce Meyer conference Saturday," my friend Jill said. "It was wonderful. I watch her on television every day, but she is even more inspiring in person."

"Oh, wow!" Marcy exclaimed. "I wish I could have gone. I sow into her ministry every chance I get."

"Me too," said Jill.

I was confused. "What do you mean you sow into her ministry?" The term was unfamiliar to me.

"We donate money to her ministry," Jill said. "That's seed faith."

"You have to demonstrate you have that tiny mustard seed of faith," Marcy chimed in. "Then when you pray, you can move mountains."

My friends continued to talk about the conference while I sipped my coffee and thought about what they had just told me. I was pretty sure I had faith as big as a tiny mustard seed. I prayed nearly every day for needs great and small, how could I not?

But I hadn't yet moved a mountain.

After my husband and I made the decision I would be an at-home mom, money was tight in our household and we had to be careful. Nevertheless, we tried to be generous. We helped out family and friends whenever we could. I always donated the kids' outgrown clothes to charity and regularly gave canned goods to the food bank. We even gave a monthly pledge to our church. *Perhaps* I thought, *we aren't sowing "seed faith" in the right places.*

I was still pondering all this the next day while I was weeding my garden. I just didn't feel comfortable with the idea God answered prayers in exchange for money gifts.

As I pulled weeds and gently loosened the soil around each plant, I marveled at how strong and sturdy my bean seedlings had become in just a couple of short weeks. Kneeling there between a row of beans and a row of corn, with rich black earth caked underneath my fingernails, I suddenly had an insight. Seeds only grow if you plant them.

My mustard seed of faith had to be planted in good soil before it would grow enough to move mountains. And what better soil than my own heart? Kneeling right there, in grubby jeans and my hair sticking out in wisps from beneath a sweat soaked bandana, I offered my heart as soil to God and asked Him to till that soil and plant a seed of faith within. I also asked Him to tend and nurture the seedling, and I promised to listen for His instructions.

Then I went on with my chores, happily confident that now my faith would grow and eventually my mountains would move.

Summer and Fall came and went. My garden yielded a bountiful harvest. I canned and froze what we couldn't use fresh, thanking God for His generous provision. Since the time I had prayed while kneeling in the dirt, I felt my relationship with God had steadily grown. But I still wasn't sure about moving mountains.

Then that Christmas, I prayed, and a mountain (well perhaps only a hill) did move.

A close friend and I liked to exchange Christmas gifts for our children. We kept up this tradition even after Marianne's husband's work moved them to a state on the other side of the country. Marianne is a very organized person, so her packages always arrived well before Christmas. Mine were usually late.

As I stood in line with my package the day before Christmas Eve I prayed, "Holy Father God, if you could arrange with Caesar Augustus for a census at just the right time for Jesus to be born in Bethlehem to fulfill prophesy, surely you can do something with the United States Post Office to get this package delivered by Christmas."

I left the Post Office believing God would take care of my package to Marianne.

Christmas Eve Marianne telephoned. "Tell me what kind of an 'in' you have with the Post Office," she said. "Your package just came, and it was postmarked only yesterday!"

I laughed. "I don't have an 'in' with the Post Office. I have an 'in' with someone much bigger." Then I proceeded to tell her about mustard seed faith and how, when it is sown in the right soil, it can grow into something marvelous.

Since that time, I've grown bolder in prayer and have seen God do some amazing things beyond what I could have dreamed. The Post Office prayer was like moving a hill, but now I've seen some mountain-sized problems moved through prayer. If you want to see some mountain-sized answers in your own life, why not start with a small hill?

Thank You Note

Thank you Holy Father God
for the parable of the mustard seed
and what Jesus taught me through it.
Thank you for sowing that tiny seed
into my open and willing heart.
Thank you for tending it there
until I was able to reap a harvest
of mountain-moving faith.

Finding Faith

KATIE AND I SAT IN THE SHADE and talked while our children enjoyed the playground. We had only been there a short time when her son Josh came running up grinning with excitement.

"Look!" He shouted. "I found a five-dollar bill."

"Where was it?" Katie asked.

"It was buried in the sand by the swing set."

Katie suggested Josh ask the handful of adults pushing young children on the swings if any of them had lost it.

"Aw, Mom," he said. "What about finders' keepers?"

"That might be someone's lunch money, Josh," she said firmly. "Now go ask around the playground and see."

Dutifully, Josh asked everyone by the swing sets. Then, for good measure, he asked everyone else at the playground, but no one claimed the five-dollar bill. When he came back, Katie told him he could keep it.

"Wow! I've been praying for some extra money," he said. "Now I can get the Lego set I've been saving for."

Katie shook her head and looked at me. "How do you explain to a kid God doesn't answer prayers like that?"

"But He does," I said.

Her eyebrows arched. "Surely, you don't believe God put that bill in the sand for Josh to find."

"Why not?"

Katie shook her head. "I'm sorry. I just can't buy that."

"Okay, then try this. That bill was buried in the sand and God uncovered it so Josh could find it."

"That could happen," Katie agreed.

"I think God uses prayers like Josh's to grow our faith," I said. "If a kid never gets a five-dollar answer to prayer, how can he have faith in time of need to ask for five hundred or even five thousand dollars as an adult?"

"Maybe so," Katie said. "But praying for things makes me uncomfortable."

I laughed. Only a few years ago I had felt the same way. However, life got a lot more complicated after the birth of my twins. Things which had been easy with one small child were far more difficult with one small child plus two babies. I told Katie about the day I had an important errand to run for my husband. "I felt really silly asking God for a parking place in front of the business. But there it was, almost like it had been reserved for me."

"Surely you're kidding," Katie said. "Street parking downtown is impossible."

"Not kidding at all. There was even half an hour's time left on the parking meter."

"Okay, but how do you know that wasn't just a coincidence?"

"Well, since then, I've kind of made a habit of asking for little things like that, and you'd be surprised how often God comes through."

Katie looked at me to see if I was serious. "Do you always get what you ask for?"

I shook my head. "No, but when I don't, I've discovered either I really didn't need it, or I wasn't paying attention."

Katie became thoughtful as we sat watching the kids at play for a while. Finally, she said, "I think I might try it. Praying, that is. My faith sure could use a boost."

Silently, I thanked Holy Father God for using a small boy to help my friend find faith. Then I thanked Him for helping me to maintain my own faith. Finding faith is a life-long journey that begins one step at a time.

Thank You Note

Thank you Holy Father God
for giving me the courage
to bring my needs before you.
Thank you that time and again
you have met my deepest needs
with mercy and love.
Thank you for allowing my faith to grow
out of those prayers.

Prayer Worriers

I COME FROM A LONG LINE OF WOMEN who worry. While Daddy was deployed in the South Pacific, Mother and I lived in the mountains with her parents. My early childhood was punctuated by Grandma's cries of "Don't! Watch out! Be careful!" and so on. Grandma was an epic worrier.

After World War II, we moved to the city for Daddy's work. Mother regularly purchased stacks of penny postcards. Every day, she faithfully wrote a few lines on one and mailed it to Grandma. "Otherwise," she explained to me, "Grandma would literally worry herself sick."

Mother herself was no slouch in the worry department. She had tremendous powers of concentration. So, no matter what else she was doing, her mind was continually turning over the problem of the day. I often turned my own worries over to her, because things she worried about always seemed to turn out okay.

"Mom, I'm worried I won't pass my math test tomorrow," I might say. And she would always reply, "Let me worry about that, and you study." I usually passed with an A. I suspect

17

handing my worry over to her allowed me to really study and concentrate on what I'd learned when I took the test.

It wasn't until I was older that I realized Mom's worrying was actually her way of praying. Unlike Grandma or Aunt Lottie, who could worry themselves into a grand tizzy, Mother's worry was purposeful. "The things I worry about seldom happen," she would say. "So, I conscientiously worry about things that could go wrong so they won't."

Marriage and children provided me plenty of opportunity, but I just didn't inherit Mother's knack for worry. Easily distracted, I would forget all about problems as soon as I was caught up in an unrelated project, or book.

Strangely enough, remarkable things happened when I let God worry. Parking places materialized just as I pulled up. Lost things appeared, sometimes even before I started looking for them. Money had a way of coming in just when I needed it.

For a long time, offering up my worries was the extent of my prayer life and, sketchy as it was, God was patient with me and continued to bless it. Even after I learned other ways to pray, "Let God worry," was still my fallback prayer.

Offering my worries up to God has given me a sense of peace and freedom throughout all the seasons of my prayer life. When I turn the problem over to God, I trust Him to get the job done. More importantly, I let Him do it His way.

Thank You Note

Thank you Holy Father God
that you don't require beautiful, crafted prayers
in Elizabethan English to respond to my needs.
Thank you that you hear my beginner prayers,
clumsy prayers, unspoken prayers, even worry prayers.
Thank you for hearing them all
and answering according to my true need,
not according to my own understanding.

The Cat
Came Back

"DON'T WORRY HONEY," my husband John said as he left for work. "That old cat knows where his food is. George will come home."

"Hope so," I whispered to myself. This was a troubling break in George's routine. He spent his nights on the town hunting and occasionally fighting, but he was usually waiting on the back steps come morning.

George was an old reprobate of a tomcat I had rescued, neutered and tried to turn into a pet. A handsome big fellow with smoky blue-gray fur and jade green eyes, he only bore a few noticeable scars from his life as a stray. Normally he was content to sleep off his adventures by day in the sunny window or his favorite chair, but at night he couldn't be kept in no matter what. Yet George always came home for breakfast.

I carried a can of cat food and a spoon to the back door. "Here Kitty, Kitty, Kitty, Tuuuuuuna fish!" I banged on the can with the spoon. That always brought him running if he was dawdling somewhere. I looked up and down the alley. Still no George.

21

Fearing the worst, I fought back tears and called my mother. "I don't know what to do. George didn't come home for breakfast today and I have to go to work."

Mother's voice was soothing. "Oh, Sweetie, I know how much you love that old cat, but don't panic. He probably just wandered a little further than usual last night. George is a survivor."

She was right. George was a survivor, but fear still gripped my heart. "I'm afraid he might be hurt and not be able to get home," I said, my voice breaking. "And I can't skip work today to go looking for him."

"You go on to work and let me worry about George, Sweetie. I'm sure he'll be okay."

No matter what else she was doing, Mother's mind was continually turning over the problem of the day. So I felt good about turning my worry about George over to her.

Still, I called George one last time and waited for an answering yowl. When none came, I headed to work where a busy day awaited me. I was working on a cookbook for one of the agency's biggest clients and the recipes were back from the test kitchen. I had to go over them with a fine-tooth comb before sending them out for typesetting. I tackled the job with a will, but my mind kept straying back to George throughout the day. I hoped he would be waiting for me when I got home.

Late that afternoon my desk phone rang. It was Mother. "Sweetie," she said, "your George has gotten himself shut up somewhere. When you get home go up and down the alley calling him and listen carefully for him to answer. He'll let you know where he is."

"Thanks, Mom. I'll let you know when I find him." Mother's confidence inspired me. I hung up and hurried through the last few recipes. Then I left for the day.

At home, I quickly grabbed the tuna can and spoon and headed out the back door. Jan next door saw me walking down the alley banging on the can and yelling, "Tuuuuuna fish."

"Looking for that big gray cat of yours?" She called out.

"Yes, he didn't come home for breakfast."

"I saw him poking around Mrs. Harris' shed when I took out our trash last night. You might check there."

I hurried to Mrs. Harris' back gate and called "Here Kitty, Kitty, Kitty!"

A mighty yowl answered. George was indeed shut in Mrs. Harris' locked shed, and he was unhappy about it. I ran up to my elderly neighbor's back door and banged on it.

Mrs. Harris opened the door a crack and peered out. "Sarah!" She looked startled. "Why are you banging at my back door?"

"My cat is in your shed," I cried. "I need to get him out!"

"Oh, my, yes! Let me find the key." While rummaging in her junk drawer for the key, Mrs. Harris explained her grandson had come to help in her garden yesterday and had locked the shed after having supper with her.

George was still yowling when the shed door opened. He marched out tail twitching. He seemed to be saying, "What took you so long?" I quickly thanked Mrs. Harris and followed him up the alley toward home where he waited on the back steps for me to let him in. He ate a double portion of tuna for supper while I called Mother.

"I worried and worried," she said. "Then it came to me what had happened. I'm so happy he's home."

George finished his dinner and jumped up in his chair. After a perfunctory grooming session, he curled up and went to sleep. "Glad you're home," I said stroking his soft fur. "And don't even think about going out tonight."

While I changed my clothes and fixed dinner, I pondered Mother's theory of worry. It was her way of praying without ceasing, I decided, and as odd as it was, our God, of His goodness and mercy, honored it. I believe that whenever the heart is turned toward God, the prayer that comes from that heart is a true prayer and God will hear and honor it.

Thank You Note

Thank you, Holy Father God
that you love our animals
as much as we do.
George could have starved to death
in that shed.
Thank you for letting Mother know
where I could find him.

Green Lights all the Way

"WHY DON'T YOU GO LIE DOWN while I bring in the groceries and put them away," my husband John said. He looked concerned. I had just come home from buying a few last-minute things for the coming baby and getting a week's worth of groceries. I must have looked as tired as I felt. This pregnancy, my third, had been difficult from the start.

"It's a deal," I said. "I feel like I have baby from my diaphragm to my knees right now. My belly is so big my arms were barely long enough to push the grocery cart."

"It won't be much longer, Honey. Remember, Doc said if he doesn't come on his due date, taking his size into account, they will consider a C-section."

I groaned. "This kid had better not be late! He's due tomorrow and I'm holding him to it."

That was part of the reason I had gone shopping. I thought an afternoon on my feet might get the process going, but so far I only felt out of sorts and crampy. Recovering from a C-section while chasing after a six-year-old and twin toddlers was the last thing I wanted to do.

I laid down and propped my aching, swollen feet up on pillows. *Thank heavens Mother has Chris and the twins for the week,* I thought, *so I don't have to deal with their dinner, baths and bedtime.*

I had no sooner made myself as comfortable as possible and closed my eyes when the phone rang. We didn't have cell phones in those days, and our landline was attached to the wall in the hallway. Since John was still bringing in groceries, I stood up to get it. I didn't even have a chance to say "Hi" when I felt a contraction and my water broke with a whoosh.

"Oh no!" I cried.

My startled friend on the other end cried out too. "What's wrong!"

"My water just broke." I stood there, phone in hand, staring in amazement at the puddle spreading on my hardwood floor as I felt another contraction.

"Have the contractions started yet?"

"Yes."

"How far apart?"

"I don't know. It's hard to tell where one leaves off and the next one starts."

My friend's voice rose several notches. "Hang up the phone and head for the hospital!" Then the line went dead.

I was still holding the phone when John walked into the hall. "What happened," he said, looking at the puddle on the floor.

"My water broke."

He grabbed the phone from me. "I'll call Dr. Bartee while you get to the car."

"But I have to clean up this mess and change my clothes."

"I'll throw down some towels," John said. "Just head for the car. We've got a lot of miles and dozens of traffic lights between us and St. Luke's."

I did as he asked. The contractions were getting stronger by the minute, and I wasn't sure we would even make it to St. Luke's on time. When John climbed in the driver's seat, he said Doc was on his way to St. Luke's and should get there about the same time as we would.

I thought about all those dozens of traffic lights and began to worry in earnest. More water was coming with each contraction and I needed to focus on breathing to keep from crying out. I pushed the worry away and muttered my trusted fall back prayer. "Holy Father God, you worry. I'm too stressed to worry about traffic lights myself."

Every time we approached a traffic light, I repeated my "Holy Father God, you worry," prayer. I was pretty sure the difference between reaching the hospital and having this baby in the car depended on not stopping. Miraculously, every single traffic light between our home and the hospital was green.

John pulled up to the emergency room entrance and shouted, "My wife's having a baby! NOW!"

A nurse came running out with a wheelchair. By then, the cotton jumper I was wearing had wicked the moisture clear up to my shoulders. Even my T-shirt was soaked. She looked at me appraisingly and hustled me into the wheelchair. As we entered the hospital, she hollered, "Someone get the elevator and hold it. It's her fourth and I don't trust her."

In the birthing room, a cheerful nurse stripped off my wet maternity clothes and helped me into a dry gown. "Now let's check and see how far along you are," she said. As she was checking, I had a mighty contraction. "Oh, my goodness!" She cried. "You've crowned him. Try not to push. I'll be back in a minute."

She returned quickly and said, "If you can breathe through one more contraction, your doctor will be in to deliver your baby."

I was able to do as she asked, but just barely. The doctor rushed into the room just in time to catch Nicholas as he burst forth from my womb. John returned from the parking lot in time to witness his birth from the open doorway.

Later, John sat next to me on the bed while I cradled our newborn. "That was a near thing," he said. "I can't believe we didn't stop at a single traffic light. Imagine what would have happened if we had hit just one."

I smiled. "You would have had to deliver the baby. Amazing things always happen when I ask God to worry for me."

"Do you think God magically turned those lights green as we approached?" John asked as he lovingly stroked Nicky's downy head.

I shook my head. "Maybe. But imagine what a mess we could have if God interfered with the traffic lights during rush hour. Instead, I believe he did an even bigger miracle."

"What's that?"

"Well Mr. Lead Foot, he kept you calm and helped you choose your route and regulate your speed to get us to the hospital in time."

God is a God of miracles but He's also a practical God. When we turn a situation over to Him we give Him permission to deal with it His way. And His way is always best.

Thank You Note

Thank you Holy Father God
for all those green lights.
Thank you for answering my "9-1-1" prayer
and staying with us
until Nicky was safely born.

Lift up Your Hearts

THE FIRST TIME I JOINED the women's prayer group at our church I was surprised when Holly, the leader, passed out report folders. I opened up mine thinking maybe it was words to choruses we would sing.

My eyes widened. "Good Heavens!" I cried. "This will be like praying the Denver telephone directory."

I looked up and saw the others smiling. A couple of women were even nodding in agreement, but they all had their folders open ready to start.

Our pastor had asked this group to help pray for all the needs the congregation brought to him, and I decided to join because it seemed a worthwhile ministry. I never expected to see a list of names taking up several pages.

The church secretary had neatly typed out the list and thoughtfully categorized the names according to need. On the first page alone there were at least thirty or forty names for healing. The categories on other pages were broken relationships (first names only), grief, needing employment and so on. Name after name after name.

Holly quickly explained to me how it worked. Each of us would take a category, pray a general prayer for that need, and then read off the names. Two of us would share the really long lists, like the one for healing. It took the better part of an hour to get through it.

I left feeling unsettled. My husband and I belonged to a couples group where we participated in a different and more satisfying kind of prayer. We sang songs, shared scripture and even words from the Lord. People came with specific needs and the group prayed for them, often with the laying on of hands. I wasn't sure this list prayer was real prayer at all.

I made an appointment with our pastor to ask him about it.

"I know it can seem dry and tedious," Father James said. "But consider this, the Lord already knows who they are and their needs. By lifting them up to Him in prayer as a community of faith we say, "Amen," that is, "Make it so," to the prayers on the hearts of those who asked us."

"Is that how you pray?" I asked. "From a typed-out list?"

"Sometimes, yes." He looked at me thoughtfully. Then he added, "Sarah, I'm responsible for each and every soul the Lord has entrusted to my care. When I learn one has a need, I pray then and there on the spot. When possible, I pray with them."

"And then you put them on a list," I said. My remark came out sharper than I intended. I looked down at my hands, embarrassed, but when I looked back up, Father didn't seem disturbed.

He looked me in the eye. "Yes, I do put them on a list."

I did my best to keep my own expression neutral. The last thing I wanted was to start an argument about prayer with my pastor.

Smiling, he went on. "But I also put them some place more important. I put them in my heart."

I knew Father James was a very kind and compassionate man who took his duties as the shepherd of his flock seriously. Of course he would put them in his heart. That made more sense than the endless list.

"Then you must have a very full and heavy heart," I said.

"I do. But please take what I'm about to say into your heart." His face became serious. "When I celebrate Holy Communion and say 'Lift up your hearts,' I am lifting up my own heart too. I make an offering of all those needs I've put there to our Lord. I empty my heart into His."

He looked at me to make sure I was following him. "You can do that too. At Communion or whenever the Holy Spirit moves you. Empty your heart into the heart of Jesus."

I left Father's office deep in thought that day. From childhood I had responded to, "Lift up your hearts" with "We lift them up unto the Lord," without ever considering what that might mean. How do I empty my heart into the heart of Jesus?

At home I opened my Bible to search out scriptures which might apply. A note fell out with the name of a friend who had asked me for prayer a couple of weeks ago. I wrote it down and stuck it in my Bible so I wouldn't forget. Yet here I was seeing it two weeks later. I shook the Bible and several similar notes fluttered onto my desk.

I guess I have lists of my own, I thought. *And apparently I don't do a very good job of praying them.*

I gathered all those scraps of paper up into a pile. Then I picked up the notes one by one, read off the names and offered up their needs to the Lord. Finally, I asked Him to write each and every name on my own heart. I would keep them there until the Holy Spirit prompted me to empty my heart into the heart of Jesus.

Since that time, I've learned that all the things that concern me—friends, family, even my country, my church—are all packed into my heart. And when it becomes a worry to me, I need to take the time to empty all of it into the heart of Jesus. Sometimes that means making a list and praying over it.

Thank You Note

Thank you Holy Father God
for the gift of communities of faith.
Thank you that you are always happy
to hear and respond to
our prayers of agreement.
Thank you for letting us entrust
the burdens of our hearts
to the heart of Jesus.

Part Two

Got Troubles?
Try Trust.

We see the small picture,
a tiny slice of what's going on.
God sees the big picture.
His timing is perfect. His solution is sure.

Tornado Warning!

I WAS TRYING TO COME UP WITH a snappy lead for a newspaper article I was writing when my four boys, who had been playing ball in the park at the end of our street, burst through the door.

"Mommy, Mommy, come quick!" The youngest shouted. "There's a cloud that looks just like a titty hanging down."

"He's right Mom," the oldest said. "I made everyone run home. I think it's a tornado!"

I started to explain it was probably just a heavy thunder storm since we lived too close to the mountains for a tornado to form. But then the emergency sirens began to wail.

"Maybe I'd better have a look," I said. "You guys get the dog and head for the basement." Without protest they quickly started for the stairs. "And take a radio with you!" I shouted.

I asked God to protect my home and my boys and our pets. Then, journalist to the core, I quickly grabbed my camera and stepped out onto the porch.

The sky was an angry greenish gray and lumpy with potential hail. Lightning flashed and thunder boomed. There was an ominous whirlpool of clouds right over our park and what Nick had described as a "titty" was indeed hanging down.

I ignored the din of sirens and thunder and began snapping pictures. Through the long lens of my camera, I saw the appendage from the cloud grow longer and thicker as it relentlessly reached closer and closer to earth. I was so fascinated I forgot to be afraid until it made contact with the ground.

Suddenly sticks and leaves and scraps of paper swirled chaotically around me. I grabbed one of the larger bits as it sailed within inches of my face. It was a menu from the restaurant only a few blocks away.

Only then did I realize how close disaster was to our home. I thanked God my boys had the good sense to come home from the park when they saw the tornado forming.

The funnel cloud seemed to be moving away from us but wailing sirens indicated it was still on the ground. I let my big, heavy camera swing on its strap around my neck while I ran to join the boys in the basement. All four were sitting on the floor of the laundry room listening intently to the radio. The dog and both cats were with them.

Chris looked up wide-eyed and said, "It took out that restaurant on the corner of Evans and Broadway where we sometimes have breakfast!"

"I know," I said, holding out the menu I had grabbed away from the wind.

The radio announced that the funnel cloud had dissipated and damage reports were starting to come in. There were flooded streets, downed trees, and damaged roofs. The restaurant was demolished, but since it was only open through lunch, it had been closed and empty when the tornado hit. There were no reports of injuries.

The twins noticed I had my camera around my neck and asked if I had taken any good pictures. "I think so," I said, "but right now we need to give thanks to our merciful God that He kept us and our home safe today."

The youngest climbed in my lap. "You should have come downstairs with us Mommy. I was scared for you."

"I'm sorry, honey," I said. "Going out to take photos probably wasn't the smartest thing to do."

"It's okay," my little boy said. "I asked God to take care of you. And He did."

Yes, indeed. He took care of *all* of us that day.

It's a good thing to know that Holy Father God is faithful to take care of us even when we aren't taking care of ourselves.

Thank You Note

Thank you Holy Father God
for the sweet, natural faith of young children.
Thank you for answering my little boy's prayer
for my safety.
Thank you for being with my children
when I foolishly decided
it was more important
to photograph that tornado
than to take shelter with them in the storm.

Forgiving is Freeing

WHEN OUR YOUNGEST WAS BORN, my husband John traded his car in on a VW Bus for me and kept my old VW Bug, a hand-me-down from my mother, to drive himself. No way could I fit four boys, not to mention the dog, in that little Bug.

On nice days when there was no school, I would load the bus with kids, snacks, maybe Grandma or a friend, and we would explore. One day when Grandma was with us, she said, "There's a restaurant near here with an old railroad caboose converted into a dining area for kids. Let's stop and have lunch. My treat."

The caboose was attached to the back of the restaurant so you could walk right in from the dining room. The tabletops and chair seats were cheerful red, and the walls were decorated with lots of photos of steam trains. There were also lanterns and other railroad memorabilia for the children to see.

"This caboose is a great idea," I told our waitress when she brought our drinks.

"Yeah, we get a lot of families here now," she said. "You can even reserve the caboose for birthday parties."

This would be a great place to have a party for Chris' ninth birthday, I thought, the only drawback being the restaurant was a lot closer to Mother's house than ours. But with the bus and a limited guest list I decided it was doable.

"How much does it cost to have a party here?" I asked when our baskets of burgers and fries came out.

"Depends on how many kids, but basically it's their meals plus some additional for a cake and party favors. We do it all. There's a minimum of five kids."

Perfect! I thought. *I'll have seven. Our four plus three friends for Chris. That's a bus load.*

"Would you like to have your birthday here?" I asked Chris. I explained it would mean inviting only three friends.

"These are great burgers! Let's do it," he said. So I made the reservation then and there for a party at 12:30 the Saturday closest to his birthday.

The morning of the party, my husband announced he was taking the bus to help a coworker move. He had been on the road all week and had forgotten our party plans.

"John, I don't think that's going to work!" I said. "Chris' guests are due at our house by 11:45 to give us plenty of time to get to the restaurant."

John grumbled he'd do his best to be home by 11:30.

"Make sure you are," I demanded.

The guests were all at our house by 11:45. At 11:55 there was still no sign of John and the bus.

I waited five more minutes, pacing the floor, before stuffing the kids into the Bug. My youngest, Nick, was small enough to squeeze into the cargo area behind the back seat. The three guests all managed to fit on the back seat. My twins sat on the floor between their feet. The birthday boy sat up front. I scanned the road one last time, fervently hoping to see John and my bus coming home. No such luck!

I prayed for safety and favor. I asked Holy Father God to stay with us the whole twenty-minute drive from our house to the party caboose. The trip seemed to take forever in that little car stuffed to the max with excited, giggling boys.

I, on the other hand, kept expecting to hear sirens. I was sure any cop who spotted me on the highway would think I'd gone mad. He would possibly even arrest me for child abuse. I hid my fears for the sake of the birthday boy and his friends, but inside I was seething.

Thankfully, we got to the restaurant safe and sound.

Once the kids were all settled and the waitress was taking their food orders, I stepped out to call John.

"Where are you?" I growled when he answered. I lit into him, trying to keep my voice down so the kids wouldn't hear.

When I finished my rampage, John said he had come home just in time to see me turn the corner at the other end of the block. "I tried to catch your attention," he said, "but you took off like you were headed to a fire."

I paced and waited for him to at least say he was sorry.

"I did my best to get home, Honey, but moving doesn't always go as planned."

"That's no excuse!" I wasn't ready to forgive or forget. Driving on the highway with all those kids crammed into the Bug had been terrifying.

"I'll come and trade cars with you now," John said. "Calm down and enjoy the party."

Enjoy the party! Ha! I was still too angry to enjoy anything.

Back inside the caboose, the noise level had risen several notches. The restaurant had provided train whistles for party favors and the kids were making full use of them. The kids were all having a great time, but the din was giving me a headache.

I sat dipping cold French fries into a pool of ketchup and sipped a soda while our waitress, dressed in a train engineer's cap with matching striped apron, served cake and little cups of ice cream. She offered some to me but I shook my head.

When I saw John pull into the parking lot with my bus, I met him with scowl on my face. Without a word he pulled me into a warm hug. "I am so sorry, Honey."

I just wanted to cry. I loved this man with all my heart, but sometimes his inattention to family things important to me and the kids made me crazy.

"Hey, you got here safely, didn't you?" He said brushing tears off my cheeks. "Am I in time for cake?"

I sighed. "Sure, come on in."

A passel of happy kids greeted him. They told an exciting tale of stuffing a VW Bug to get to the party. "It was kinda like one of those clown cars at the circus," one boy said.

John smiled at me as he forked his cake. "Sounds like the highlight of the party, Honey."

I had to laugh. How could I stay mad? My anger had only served to steal my joy.

I acknowledged Holy Father God had protected me and the kids. I also acknowledged my impatience had led me to recklessly put all those kids in the Bug. Then I forgave John, who always tries to do the right thing by everyone. I soon felt the peace of God wash over me.

"I think I'll have some of the cake after all," I told the waitress. Then I sat back to enjoy what was left of the party.

I realized that day that I been too wrapped up in keeping to "my" plan when Holy Father God had a different plan in mind. My frustration over not being able to keep my plan had stolen my joy. I also learned that Holy Father God is faithful to His little ones. All those little boys only remember having the time of their lives. I could have enjoyed it with them instead of simmering in my own pity party.

Thank You Note

Thank you Holy Father God
for showing us we not only free the person
who has caused us harm when we forgive;
we also set ourselves free from bitterness and resentment.
Thank you for restoring relationships
and filling our hearts with joy.
Thank you for using my son's birthday
to teach me this important lesson.

Angels Without Wings

I TURNED THE KEY IN THE IGNITION. The starter motor cranked but the engine didn't start. I tried again. Same result. What had begun as a perfect late spring day for a picnic was turning out anything but.

"I know we have plenty of gas," I said to my mother. "I stopped and filled the tank just before I picked you up."

Six-year-old Chris unfastened his seat belt and came up to the front of my aging VW bus. "Why did we stop here, Mommy?"

"I don't know why the bus stopped, Chris, but I'm going to look at the engine and find out." I spoke with confidence I certainly didn't feel.

My toddler twins complained they were hungry and the baby was stirring in his car seat, so I asked my mother to try to keep the kids calm and entertained while I looked for the problem.

I grabbed a rag from the back and opened the engine compartment. I did the few things I knew how to do—checked the oil (good), the cables to the battery terminals (tight), and looked to see if any of the belts were broken or loose (nope). Then I looked down the bumpy road we had come up and tried to calculate how long it would take me to walk back to the highway.

I figured Mother could feed the kids their picnic in the bus while I went to get help and told her so. But she was already unloading the older kids and sitting them down on the embankment at the side of the road. Each was happily munching a chocolate chip cookie she had baked that morning.

"I think it would be safer for you and the kids to stay in the car while I walk back down," I said.

She just smiled and sat down with the children. The baby was on her lap, making a mess of his clothes and hers with one of the baby biscuits I had packed for him. "You're the one who's always telling me to pray, have faith and trust God," she said. "I don't think we'll have to wait very long for Him to send us an angel."

Yeah, right, I thought. *An angel mechanic who works on old VW buses. Fat chance.*

I turned back to the engine compartment and rechecked everything I had checked before. I was wiping the grease off my hands and getting ready to insist Mother put everyone back in the bus when two of her angels arrived. One drove a big truck, the other a jeep.

An older man climbed down from the truck. "Out of gas, ma'am?" he asked my mother.

"No, my daughter filled the tank this morning."

A young man got of the jeep and asked how he could help.

Angel Number One told him to get in and crank while he took a look at the engine.

"Starter motor's okay," Angel Number One said, "and plenty of juice from the battery."

Meanwhile I was looking at his truck, which had a crew cab. There would be plenty of room for him to take Mother and the kids back to town while I waited with the bus for a tow. I hoped he would be willing.

Just then Angel Number Three arrived on a trail bike.

"What's the problem?" he asked.

Angel Number One told him there was plenty of juice from the battery but the bus wouldn't start.

"Let me take a look, he said, "I used have one of these. They're easy to work on."

Angel Number Three poked around in the engine compartment and came up with a loose wire. "Here's your problem," he said. "One of your spark plug wires came off."

He replaced the wire and called to Angel Number Two. "Try cranking it now." The bus started and ran like nothing had ever been wrong.

Angel Number Three accepted my offer of the rag for his greasy hands. "Better turn around though," he said. "This road hasn't been graded yet and that wire might jiggle off again."

Angel Number One agreed as he climbed back into his truck and headed on up the road.

Angel Number Two looked anxious. "Do you think you have enough room to turn around," he said. "I could do it for you."

I was about to tell him I knew how to drive my bus when Angel Number Three said, "Oh, of course she does. This baby's turning radius is as short as your Jeep's." Then he turned to me while Angel Number Two drove off. "I'll stick around to make sure you get turned okay. You know, just in case."

I turned my bus wth no problem and headed back the way I came. Chris whined, "But what about our picnic?"

Mother turned to him and said, "It's a perfect day for a picnic, and I know a great picnic spot closer to town. It's in my backyard."

I was amazed at how calm my mother stayed in this crisis. Her capacity for worry is almost legendary. Yet this time I was the one who worried and she was the one who prayed. And Holy Father God answered her with not one, but three angels without wings.

I learned that day that Holy Father God is faithful to send help in the most unexpected ways, even when our faith is quite small.

Thank You Note

Thank you Holy Father God
that some of your angels are very human,
yet still open to lending aid.
Thank you for those three men
who were angels to us
when my bus stalled on a rough mountain road.
Thank you for my mother's calm faith
and presence of mind.

Mothers Can't be Everywhere

WHEN I SET ASIDE my advertising career to be an at-home mother, I felt I had to justify my decision by becoming the best of all possible mothers. Consequently, I assumed responsibility for the smallest details in my children's lives. If one went to school without his lunch, it was my fault for not making sure he had it. If one fell and scraped his knee, it was my fault for not monitoring his play closely enough.

I took great pride in "being there" for my four boys at all times. Other children had latch keys or went to day care after school. Mine came home to freshly baked bread or cookies. Others spent their summer at day camps, which I considered over-crowded and under-supervised. Mine had me to take them on adventures in the mountains and picnics in the park.

With that mindset, no wonder my favorite coffee mug bore the slogan, "God can't be everywhere—that's why He created mothers." I never questioned its message until a sudden and violent summer storm taught me just the opposite is true.

During school vacations, I usually planned one or two "fun" stops, like the library or ice cream parlor, into my weekly

57

errands so we could all go together. On this particular sultry August afternoon, however, all four boys were flopped in front of the TV watching one of the videos I had rented to alleviate their end-of-summer boredom.

"I have a few errands to run," I said. "Come along, and we'll get some ice cream."

My suggestion brought only groans of protest. "It's too hot, Mom. We want to stay home and finish watching the movie."

I thought it over for a moment and decided the oldest, who was twelve, was plenty old enough to supervise his brothers for the short time it would take me to go to the bank, the dry cleaners, and the grocery store.

"Okay," I said. "Chris is in charge. Be good, and I'll bring home some ice cream." Absorbed in the movie, they hardly acknowledged my leaving.

Although I rarely left the boys unsupervised for even a few minutes, I reassured myself they would be just fine and attributed the uneasy feeling churning through my mind to the unusually hot and humid weather. *I'd rather veg out this afternoon myself,* I thought, scanning the heavy gray sky. *Maybe we'll get a cooling rain by evening.*

A few big spatters of rain had indeed begun to fall while I was at the bank, and the sky grew even darker. Suspecting a thunderstorm might be coming, I decided to skip the dry cleaners and finish my grocery shopping. Mentally streamlining my list, I hurried up and down the aisles picking up only what I absolutely needed.

I was just finishing up when the storm broke.

Thunder grumbled and sheets of wind-driven rain crashed against the windows of the market. While I waited in the checkout line, I began to fret.

At first my worries were more about the household than the children. Did the boys think to let the dog in? Did they close the windows? I was afraid they would forget because they had been watching a movie. My husband and I have a standing joke that a bomb could go off when the TV was on and the boys wouldn't notice.

After I paid for my groceries, I tried to make a run for my car, even though the clerks and other customers advised me to wait. I didn't make it far. The wind and water soaked me in seconds and huge hail stones drove me back into the store. While the storm got worse instead of better, I paced and chatted with other stranded shoppers to ease my tension. One elderly couple was worried because they had left their dogs outside.

Surely the kids let Shadow in, I hoped.

Air-raid sirens began to wail, signaling this was more than a standard summer thunderstorm and a tornado warning was in effect. Panic gripped me in earnest.

The boys didn't even know where I was. My every attempt to call home was thwarted by downed phone lines. *And I always yell at them when they leave without telling me where they are going,* I thought.

Were they frightened? Were they worried about me? Had they thought to switch from video to TV to get the storm warning?

Some Mother, I am, I chastised myself. *How can I forgive myself for going off like that, when common sense should have told me a bad storm was coming? How can I even ask God to forgive me for letting them down?*

Then in the midst of my rising panic, a single line from the Psalms popped into my mind. *Be still, and know that I am God.*

I wasn't even sure which Psalm it came from at the time, but that line acted on me like a mighty tranquilizer. Somehow, deep inside, I felt absolute assurance the boys and our household would be all right.

When the sirens stopped, I headed for my car. My way home was rather treacherous. Visibility was poor, the streets were slick, cars were stalled in deep puddles and drifts of hail, but each time I started to panic, those words would come right back into my mind. *Be still, and know that I am God.*

The main street I would have normally taken home looked like a river, so I wisely headed for higher ground. Some intersections were still difficult to negotiate, and I had a near miss when the driver of another car failed to see mine, even though I had the headlights on. Finally, I pulled up in front of my house. I left the groceries in the car and ran inside.

Everything was dark and far too quiet. Fear grabbed my heart.

At first I was afraid the boys had panicked and left. But where would they have gone? Then I heard the radio in the basement. Relief washed over me as I headed down the stairs and found all four boys in the laundry room. The dog and cats were tucked in safely beside them..

"Wow, Mom!" Chris said, jumping up to greet me, "What a storm!"

"Yeah," the twins chimed in. "We were watching that movie when it suddenly got really dark."

The youngest hugged me tight, while Chris continued, "The sky turned a creepy color, and something seemed to tell me we had better let Shadow in and start shutting windows. Then we switched over to TV and heard there was a tornado watch, so we all came down here."

"I'm so proud of you," I said. "You did exactly right."

A quick check revealed they had not only remembered the safest place in the house, but they had closed all the windows, turned off lights, and even unplugged the computer and the television.

Be still, and know that I am God. (Psalm 46:10 NRSV)

"Thank you God," I whispered, "for being with my boys when I could not." Then I added, "And for being with me at the same time and for giving me peace in spite of the storm."

Later, after I mopped up the water that had come through the kitchen window before the children could get it shut, I inspected my hail-devastated garden and borrowed a neighbor's phone to report ours out of order. I felt strangely relieved rather than depressed. The phone and garden were things that could be repaired. The important thing was that all my children were safe.

I had been cramming my children's heads with instructions and warnings almost from their births. "Stay away from tall trees and water in thunderstorms." "Look both ways before crossing." "Never leave home without telling me where you are going." But I had never really trusted my children to follow through on their own. Yet when danger threatened and I was away, with the help of the Holy Spirit, they kept their heads and remembered just what to do. I was so proud of them and grateful to God.

As my boys have grown into young men, the lesson of that storm has stuck with me and helped me to be still and know that God is God through many more of life's storms.

My job, I have learned, is to teach and to give example; their job is to learn and to follow through; and God's job is to make up the difference when any one of us falls short. I have also discovered the more I learn to trust God, the more I am able to trust my children as well. They don't always have the best judgment, nor do they always make the right decisions, but they do learn and grow, and they do give their father and me far more occasions for joy than sorrow.

I no longer use the "God can't be everywhere..." mug. I actually dropped it from a second floor window onto the hard cement patio below, and then swept up the pieces and threw them in the trash.

My new mug says, "This is the day which the LORD has made; let us rejoice and be glad in it." (Psalm 118:24 NRSV)

Now, when I drink my morning coffee, I am reminded daily to take my focus off me and put it where it belongs—on God the Father, Son, and Holy Spirit. I rejoice that He is God. Moms can truly only be in one place at one time, but God *is* everywhere at all times and in every situation.

Thank You Note

Thank you Holy Father God
that it doesn't ever all depend upon me.
Thank you that you make up
for what I lack as a parent.
Thank you for being present
in every moment of our lives.

Miracles
do Happen

ALL OF MY MOTHER INSTINCTS told me to pick up the baby that was crying, but my eyes told me the baby lying quietly on the floor was the one in trouble. He was pale and still. A great purple lump was swelling on his forehead where he had hit the aquarium stand.

Just moments before, I had watched in delight, as my year-old twins, Billy and Danny, pulled themselves up to see the colorful fish in our aquarium. They stood giggling and pointing for two or three minutes. Then Billy lost his balance and came down hard on the seat of his pants, upsetting his brother as he fell. Startled, Billy began to cry, but Danny, who fell against the corner of the heavy aquarium stand, was knocked unconscious and just quietly crumpled to the floor.

Too frightened to give it much thought, I scooped Billy up with my right arm to quiet him, then put my left hand over Danny's bruised temple and said aloud, "Holy Father God, I can't do anything about this. You can!"

Danny opened his eyes and smiled at me. He never even cried. His color came back and he started to sit up. When I took my hand away, there was only a faint red spot where the ugly purple bruise had been.

This happened when the charismatic renewal was going full swing in our church. I had seen many wonderful things happen in the prayer group my husband and I attended, but this was the first time God had ever used me to do His work of healing. Enormously grateful and excited beyond measure, I told everybody who would listen about the wonderful healing miracle which had taken place in our living room.

Somewhere in the telling and retelling of the story, however, something went wrong. The emphasis shifted from praising God, who had done the miracle, to the gift of healing, and then to me. "I feel sure you must have a healing ministry," one earnest friend told me. Another encouraged me to learn all I could about prayer for healing and even gave me a list of books. Still others simply asked me to pray for them, which I did, with varying degrees of success.

I decided that either healing was a very fickle gift or I did not know enough about it to use it effectively. So I dived into that book list. I not only read the late Agnes Sanford's classic, *The Healing Light*, I also read every other book she wrote. I zealously searched the *Bible* for passages that had to do with healing. As I read and studied, I tried to come up with a foolproof method, a formula for healing prayer that would always work. But still my gift proved fickle.

Perhaps I'm not holy enough, I thought. So with the same zeal I had put into study, I undertook a holiness program. I began to go to church not only every Sunday but also every service offered during the week as well. I added a Bible study and another prayer group to my weekly agenda. I set aside regular prayer times at home both morning and evening. God blessed my efforts by drawing me into a relationship with Him unlike anything I had ever experienced before. My gift of healing, however, became, if anything, even less reliable.

"Perhaps I'm not healed enough," was my next thought. In spite of all that prayer and study, a very unscriptural idea had taken root in my mind that a healer should be an example of health in body, mind and spirit. Since I have been given a remarkably disease-resistant body, I began first to seek inner healing for my mind and spirit. As I explored the pain of my past with the help of a wise and loving counselor and spiritual mentor, I grew even closer in my relationship with my Holy Father God. Yet my gift of healing continued erratic.

Years passed, and at some point I just set the gift of healing aside. Whenever a group laid hands on someone for healing, I didn't hesitate to join in, but I no longer thought of myself as a healer. Occasionally, someone would still request that I lay hands upon them, but I always prefaced my prayer with a disclaimer: "Sometimes this works when I do it, and sometimes it doesn't."

Then, during a Thanksgiving Day dinner my church sponsored for the poor, the homeless, and the lonely, I noticed a youth sitting in a corner with a cast on his arm and pain in his eyes. He was the son of one of the volunteers helping serve. I went over and asked what had happened.

He told me his name was Davy and he had sustained a spiral fracture while sledding the day before. "The doctor said I'll be in this cast at least fifteen weeks," he said bravely, trying to look as though it were nothing. "I might need surgery. He'll check again in a week to see." Then, he added, "It hurts a lot."

"I'll bet it does," I said, and without thinking about it, offered, "Would you like me to lay hands on your arm and pray?" He nodded that he would.

Silently, I began to pray: "Holy Father God, I feel so bad for this precious child of yours. He's really hurting and there is nothing I can do to make it better. But I know YOU can. Please help." Then I prayed something more out loud, but I'm not sure what, because suddenly I felt a pair of invisible hands come down on top of my hands, and the heat of them went right through into Davy's arm.

We both sat there, caught up in the wonder of the moment, until, as suddenly as it had begun, the heat died away.

"Should I take the cast off?" he asked, wide-eyed.

"No. God works through doctors and medicine, too," I said. "But, please, ask your Mom to call me after your doctor's appointment next week."

When she did, the news was good. "Praise God!" she shouted. "The doctor was amazed. He said the break was healing faster and better than he had dared to hope. And the cast should come off in only two more weeks."

I praise my Holy Father God for Davy's healing. I also praise Father, Son and Holy Spirit for using this healing to show me why the more I tried to strengthen my gift of healing, the less reliable it became. As St. Paul put it in 2 Corinthians 12:10 (NRSV) ". . . when I am weak, then I am strong." I now understand the most powerful prayer we have, in the name of Jesus, is the prayer that acknowledges our awesome God's strength and our own weakness, the prayer that says, "Holy Father God, I can't. You can!"

Thank You Note

Thank you Holy Father God
that your strength is manifest in our weakness.
Thank you that your help is available
whenever we find ourselves helpless.
Thank you also for allowing us
to be your partners in miracles of healing.

Gone in a Heartbeat

NO MATTER HOW HARD the hospital tries to make their rooms cheerful and comfortable, the surgery waiting room always seems sad and bleak to me. I still struggle with all those hard memories of waiting with my mother during Daddy's surgery, which ended in his death. Those memories came tumbling back the morning I waited while my own husband had open heart bypass surgery.

My earliest memory of Daddy was the day he came home from war. I was three years old. I also remember nights while he was away when Mother would sit with me and pray for him to come home safe. And he did!

Daddy came home and gave me a red wagon and new shoes. What could be a better answer to a little girl's prayer than that?

What Mother didn't tell me was that Daddy came home because he had been very sick. He spent months hospitalized, first in the Philippines and then stateside, recovering from a nasty tropical lung infection that damaged the valve between his heart and his lungs.

Yet, throughout my childhood, Daddy seemed healthy and active. I was Daddy's girl and we did all kinds of special things together. A master marksman himself, he gave me my first .22 rifle and showed me how to shoot. He taught me to burn my gold pan black in a campfire so the flecks of gold would show up when I panned the abandoned dredge ponds near our mountain home. He took me hiking and made sure I knew how to find my way in the woods.

I was devastated when he sold our mountain house in 1961 because he could no longer handle the high altitude. Busy with friends and my own senior year high school activities, I hadn't been paying attention to the many signs Daddy's heart was slowly giving out.

By the time he walked me down the aisle to marry John in 1966, he had slowed down considerably. Only a year later, Mother confided it was hard for him to even walk to the end of the driveway.

I was heartbroken. I was afraid I might lose the strong, handsome Daddy who continued to be a mentor even after my marriage. He advised John and me on so many things, like purchasing our first house. I was also looking forward to seeing Daddy as a grandfather. I wanted him to teach my children all the special things he had taught me.

Surgeons were implanting artificial heart valves with some success in the early sixties. Daddy and his cardiologist discussed the possibility and decided the many associated problems made this a poor option in his case. Then in 1968 a French cardiologist developed a way to preserve a pig heart valve with formalin for implantation in humans.

Dr. Schoonmaker, Daddy's cardiologist, studied the procedure in detail before telling Daddy about it. My father knew this surgery was very new and very risky. But he also knew he was dying. He hoped this surgery would give him a chance to live. I prayed he was right.

A year after it's introduction, in August, 1969, Daddy had surgery to replace his faulty heart valve with a pig valve. He died in recovery. He was only 54 years old.

Less than a year later I gave birth to Daddy's first grandchild in the same hospital. Every time I heard Dr. Schoonmaker paged I started to cry. The nurses thought I was suffering from post partum depression. But I was still deep in grief. I had just given Daddy a grandson he would never see, never take shooting, never teach how to find his way in the woods.

My husband John was a father after my Daddy's heart. He regularly took our four children hiking, camping and fishing. His father was a good grandfather to them too. But for me there was always a lingering sadness that Daddy wasn't there to show them how to pan for gold or shoot clay pigeons.

Intellectually, I knew comparing John's surgery with Daddy's surgery was comparing apples and oranges, but emotionally I couldn't quite get past it. I was terrified I could lose John in surgery the way I had lost my father.

"Holy Father God," I prayed, "there's nothing I can do. It's all in your hands. You've taken my Daddy. Please don't take my husband as well."

Dr. Barclay, John's surgeon finally came out.

"He did well. He's in recovery now," he said. He pulled up a chair. Then he made a rough drawing of John's heart and showed me what he had done.

I paid attention. I nodded in all the right places. All the while thinking of Daddy. And how his surgery hadn't been quite so simple.

"My father had open heart surgery," I suddenly blurted out.

Dr. Barclay straightened. "He did? When? Was it here?"

"At St. Luke's," I said. "In 1969."

Dr. Barclay's eyebrows lifted. "Who was his cardiologist?"

"Dr. Schoonmaker," I said. "He replaced Daddy's faulty heart valve with a pig valve. We thought it would give him a chance to live." I blinked back tears.

Dr. Barclay reached across the table and touched my hand. "I studied under Dr. Schoonmaker. He was a brilliant cardiologist. A pioneer," he said. "And your father was a very brave man."

"But he died," I whispered.

"Yes," Dr. Barclay said, "But because of his courage, countless others live. That surgery was new then. Now it's done successfully all over the world. We are grateful for those like your father who were willing to take the risk so we could perfect the procedure."

I just nodded, too emotional to trust myself to speak. I'd never thought of it that way.

I realized then that all those years between Daddy's heart surgery and John's, I had been harboring a deep failure to trust. I didn't trust my Holy Father God to work through doctors and medical means for healing. Yet in truth God was very much at work in surgeries and many other procedures, and He had been at work in Daddy's death.

My father's death had been inevitable, but Holy Father God had used his death to help others. My father had made the brave choice, knowing others would benefit and also knowing he would spend eternity with God.

As these thoughts came to me, I realized I could make the brave choice to trust Holy Father God as well. And hadn't He just come through in a beautiful way with my husband John?

Thank You Note

Thank you Holy Father God
for bringing my husband safely
through open heart surgery,
and so granting him many more years of life.
Thank you also for using my father's sacrifice
of his life to save the lives of many others
throughout the world.
Thank you for working
through doctors and medicine
to grant healing.

Wilderness Rescue

MY HUSBAND JOHN AND I celebrated our recently emptied nest by purchasing a four-wheel drive vehicle equipped for off-road. We were eager to explore some of the back country we had long wanted to see but never had with our family. There are many places in the Colorado Rockies where a VW Bus stuffed with kids, dog, and camping gear just shouldn't go.

On one trip, we invited our friends, Bud and Donna, to come along. After a day of four-wheeling, we decided to have dinner in Walden, a small town in rural northern Colorado near the Wyoming border, rather than go back to camp.

The late afternoon sun shimmered on the pavement as we drove along the open road. We passed through open range where cattle were grazing, and we hadn't seen another car for miles. Our dogs were asleep in the cargo area, while the four of us chatted happily about the places we had been that day. My husband was our driver and was relaying a story when he suddenly dropped out of the conversation.

I was looking at Donna and wondered what had distracted him. "John?" I said.

I turned and saw his eyes were wide open and staring straight ahead. His knuckles were white as he gripped the wheel. The car began to drift to the side of the road.

"John!" I shouted.

But he did not respond. Instead, his body began to jerk and our SUV slid off the side of the road. It seemed like it rolled forever, but in reality, it rolled three times down an embankment, coming to rest on its wheels in the dry grass. The engine was still running, and I could smell raw gasoline.

Terrified the grass would catch fire and we would be trapped inside, I reached to turn off the engine. Excruciating pain pulled me back and I drew in a sharp breath. I soon realized my right arm was broken. Probably in shock, I managed to turn the key with my left hand instead. Then I took an assessment of our situation.

John was unconscious and bleeding from a vicious head wound; Donna was in shock; and Bud, the least hurt of all of us, was on his cell phone trying to get help. But we were too far out and there was no service. My heart raced and I felt panic beginning to rise. I knew I would be of no help to my dear husband if I panicked, so I cried out to God.

Suddenly, a single Bible verse popped into my head and hung there like a shining promise. It's where Joseph says to his brothers, "As for you, you meant evil against me; but God meant it for good . . ." Genesis 50:20 (NRSV). In that brief moment, I remembered Joseph's brothers abandoned him in a wilderness pit and he had to trust God to bring him safely out. Like Joseph, I too had to trust God to bring us safely out of our desperate situation.

I placed my left hand over John's right hand feeling a good pulse. He was still with me. Then, I began to simply pray, "We're hurt and helpless in the middle of nowhere Holy Father God. Please send help."

Then I blinked tears from my eyes and tried hard to trust help was on its way.

God answered my prayer in such a spectacular way that when I told people about it later, they had trouble believing it was true. But the truth is, on that lonely stretch of highway where we hadn't seen another vehicle, and within minutes of the accident, another car came along in answer to my prayer. And as if that wasn't enough, God had placed four paramedics inside that car. They were returning home from a training class in Wyoming.

After quickly assessing the situation, they radioed for an ambulance. One of the paramedics worked to staunch the bleeding from John's head wound and stabilize him. Another immobilized my broken arm. "How did this happen?" he asked.

I explained John's odd behavior and how he jerked the wheel when I shouted his name.

"Is he epileptic?" the paramedic asked. "It sounds like he might have had a *grand mal* seizure."

I shook my head. "Not that we know."

"Be sure to tell the doctors at the hospital what you just told me," he said. "It could be important."

Our rescuers treated Donna for shock and immobilized her broken ankle. They also calmed and reassured Bud while they treated the scratches and bruises he had sustained. By then the ambulance from Walden arrived and we were loaded in.

I learned later, that after seeing us all on the way to the nearest hospital, the first paramedics on the scene gathered up our dogs, Frisco and Cherokee, who both miraculously survived but needed medical care. The paramedics graciously took them to the nearest veterinary clinic.

Answers to prayer continued to come in for months following our accident. Once I knew all four of us and both dogs were on their way to recovery, I began praying about material things.

I asked Holy Father God to grant us the means to purchase a vehicle to replace the SUV we had wrecked. We had taken out a hefty loan to buy that off-road rig, and friends cautioned us our insurance would probably not pay it off in full. Yet once the claim was settled, we owed nothing on the SUV and had enough money left over to buy a serviceable used car.

Holy Father God took care of Donna too. She had been concerned all summer about returning to her job as a school lunchroom manager. The long hours on her feet and heavy lifting were beginning to take a toll. Her foot and ankle injury in the accident made returning to that job impossible. God, through our insurance, provided a retraining program which enabled her to land a much better desk job.

Tests revealed John, indeed, had a seizure disorder which could be controlled through medication. This spared him from conviction of careless driving and a hefty fine. It also meant I had to grow in confidence and skill as a driver so I could take over driving in extreme light conditions, like the shimmer of sun on pavement, which could trigger his seizures.

That accident changed our lives forever, but change, while sometimes difficult to accept, is not necessarily bad. Looking back, I can see many ways God did for us what He had done for Joseph when he redeemed the treachery of Joseph's brothers. Today, I can truly say what the ancient enemy of mankind intended to use for evil when our SUV rolled down that embankment, our Holy Father God used for good.

It still hurts me to talk about that accident and think of how close I came to losing John, but whenever my thoughts drift there, I fast forward to the amazing arrival of those four paramedics in answer to my prayer. Yes, we were months in the healing process, but throughout it all God was with us. We would have never known how sufficiently He can meet our needs if we hadn't needed Him in such a big way.

I learned through that situation that God answers even the smallest of heartfelt prayers.

Thank You Note

Thank you Holy Father God
for bringing good out of circumstances
that look like disasters to us.
Thank you for being with John,
myself, and our friends in that accident
and preserving all our lives,
and even the lives of our dogs.
Thank you for sending immediate help within minutes
and wonder of wonders
help with medical knowledge and skill.

Part Three

God Listens.
Do We?

A still small voice, an unexpected offer of help,
a verse in the Bible, a word from a friend.
God has many ways of speaking.
Let's not miss His message.

The Dog Who Wouldn't Let Me Give up

AFTER OUR AUTOMOBILE ACCIDENT, a paramedic told me our dog Frisco had been found and taken to a veterinarian. Frisco couldn't stand up and the future didn't look good for him.

Beyond all the hurts in my body and all my worries for John, my heart hurt for that dog. He was family. Once I knew John would be okay, I spent much of the evening in prayer for Frisco.

Frisco came home from the veterinary hospital the day after I was released from rehab. His right front leg where the nerves had been crushed beyond repair was amputated. I had a broken arm, a surgically repaired shoulder, and a pinched nerve in my back. Walking was difficult and painful. Together, we started to heal.

While Frisco's physical injuries were more serious, I was the one whose spirit was broken. I sat for hours wondering if I would ever resume normal activities. It depressed me to think that camping, hiking, and enjoying the mountains might be lost to me forever.

While I brooded, Frisco would gamely struggle to his feet and lay his head in my lap to comfort me. He wasn't giving up on life, and he wasn't going to let me give up either.

"Look!" my physical therapist exclaimed a few days after our homecoming. "Frisco is already adapting to having only three legs."

Sure enough, Frisco was standing with his remaining front leg centered to balance his weight. He wagged his tail when the doctor suggested a short walk for me, as though to say, "Can I come too?" I snapped on his leash and, with the therapist helping, we walked to the end of the block and back.

Throughout that fall and winter, Frisco and I continued walking, going further and further as we both grew stronger.

By spring, I thought we might be ready to try an easy hike. I poured over my trail books and finally picked a so-called *easy* trail not far from home.

On a glorious spring day, I packed a picnic. Then my husband John, Frisco, and I jumped in the car and headed out. The snow had melted from the foothills, and the grass was lush and green. The first leg of the trail took us through a gentle meadow where pale purple butterfly lilies poked through tall grass. Pink clover and nodding harebells released sweet scents into the air, making me glad we had chosen just such a day for our hike.

After crossing the meadow, the trail headed into a stand of pines and plunged down a steep embankment toward a little creek.

"Uh oh," I said. "I hope there's an easy climb out."

John looked at me with concern. "Do you want to turn back?"

"No way," I said. "I've been looking forward to this hike for days." My bold words belied my fear. I knew better than to trust a trail that started going downhill. Going down was no problem. But coming back up was another matter.

A log bridge led us across the creek that was swift and cold with spring runoff. The trail meandered beside the creek for a mile or so.

I let Frisco off the leash. With three legs it was better for him to choose his own path and set his own pace. He was a good dog who came immediately whenever called and never chased wildlife.

Neither John nor I were in a hurry. A light breeze rippled the aspen leaves and filled the air with the vanilla scent of pinyon pine. Only a few puffy white clouds dotted the sky, while Indian paintbrushes, black-eyed Susan's, and blue sky pilots spread a carpet around us. Beside the stream little white violets were tucked in here and there between the rocks.

I didn't start to feel anxious until the sides of the little canyon grew much steeper. I still felt good, however, and Frisco was having no trouble keeping up, plus I knew the trail looped back to the parking lot. I figured we didn't have much further to go.

The trail crossed the creek again and started up the hillside. A blue jay screeched his indignation at our intrusion from a nearby aspen, and a sassy pine squirrel chattered in agreement. The first switchback was a gentle side hill climb that presented no difficulty. I was able to keep up with John whose legs were longer and stronger. Frisco was having a wonderful time. He bounded ahead, checking out all the things that interest dogs, then he doubled back to check on me before heading off again.

On the second, steeper switchback, I began to lag behind.

John suggested we stop and rest, which I gratefully accepted. We sat on the bank while I caught my breath. Then we stood and climbed some more. I kept telling myself the car was just a little further on, but before I knew it, John and Frisco got quite a bit ahead of me. I was amazed at the way Frisco, his tail waving, negotiated the steep trail with his strange, hopping, three-legged gait. It didn't seem to bother him at all. While I, on the other hand, was having trouble getting my breath.

Then switchback number three came into sight.

I stopped.

It was even steeper than the hill we had come down. And it was littered with rocks and loose gravel. There was no way I could make it up. I sat down on a big rock and tried to keep from crying. My back ached, my knee joints hurt, and my left foot had gone numb.

Holy Father God, how in the world am I going to make it out of here?

I felt stupid for having tried this hike. I asked God to send help, although I couldn't imagine what kind of help could rescue me so far out in the wilderness. Perhaps the forest ranger on an ATV? Or a young, strong hiker who could put me in a fireman's carry on his back? That thought almost made me laugh.

Please God, I really do need help.

Help came quickly, but not in any way I could have imagined.

Frisco came running back down the trail and sat down beside me. Clearly, he wasn't going to leave me behind. John called from the top that our car was in sight.

Frisco let me rest a while, and then he went up the trail a short way, turned around, and barked at me to follow. He was saying, "Look, if I can do it with only three legs, you can do it too."

I managed to stand up and carefully plant one foot after the other sideways in the loose gravel until I made it to where he waited. I grabbed onto a sapling by the side of the trail for support and looked up to John.

"It's not far to the car from here," he called.

Frisco let me rest again for a moment, and then repeated his performance. That way, a few feet at a time, we climbed the rest of the hill. Once I was walking on level ground again, my pain and tension let up.

Back at the car, I gave Frisco water and rewarded him with a treat. Then I relaxed and sat on the back of the car with John while we enjoyed our sandwiches.

I learned from that experience God does send help when we ask for it even when the situation looks impossible. Often that help comes in ways we don't expect. It may even come through our four-legged friends.

Thank You Note

Thank you Holy Father God
for my loyal and courageous three-legged dog
who helped me climb that hill.
Thank you for the special blessing
you have given us in the animals
who become our companions.

One Baby
Two Mothers

"CHRIS," I YELLED, hoping my four-year-old would hear me over the Sesame Street video he was watching. I was about to call out again when he knocked on the bathroom door.

"What do you need, Mommy?" He asked.

"Please run next door and tell Aunt Joanie I need some help."

"I'm a big boy now, Mommy. I can help you." He sounded eager.

"You're a wonderful helper, Honey." I tried to keep my voice calm. I didn't want to frighten Chris. "You help me with lots of things. But this time Mommy really needs Aunt Joanie."

"Okay, I'll go get her."

Joan and I had gotten to know each other one Sunday morning over coffee and doughnuts after church. We were close to the same age. We discovered we were neighbors and also shared a lot of interests in common like baking and needlework. It wasn't long before we were close friends.

Now I was nine months pregnant with twins and almost as big around as I was tall. (Sixty inches if you must know.) I had decided to relax in a nice warm bath while Chris watched a

93

video. When the water started to get cold, I pulled the plug and tried to get up, but I had foolishly taken the rubber tub mat out because it was uncomfortable to sit on. Try as I might, I couldn't get up and out of the slippery tub. I sat there shivering with a towel draped over my shoulders and fought tears while Chris went to get Joan.

Soon Joan knocked on the bathroom door. "Sarah, are you okay?" Her voice was filled with concern.

I heaved a sigh of relief. With a little help I thought I could get up without calling 911 and having probably male paramedics see me in the all together.

"I'm stuck, Joan. I took a bath and can't get out of the tub."

"You can't get out of the tub!"

I thought I heard her stifle a laugh. *Why not,* I thought. *When I'm out of this predicament, I'll probably be laughing too.*

"Okay," she said. "I'm coming in."

With Joan's arms around me, I managed to get on my feet and out of the tub. She helped me dry and get dressed. Then we did have a good laugh.

Throughout my twin pregnancy Joan helped out in many ways, often bringing over a meal or entertaining Chris to give me some time for myself. She even came over in the mornings to tie my shoes when I could no longer reach over my belly.

Joan continued to be wonderful help and support after Billy and Danny were born. I felt truly blessed to have found such a good friend in my neighbor. She was the only one in my circle of friends who wasn't too intimidated to babysit a pair of breastfed babies. When the twins were a little more than a year old, Joan babysat for me while I went for my annual checkup. In my doctor's office I received some shocking and quite unexpected news. I was pregnant again.

"How could that happen!" I exclaimed. "I'm still nursing both babies."

My doctor smiled. "You're not the first woman to be fooled by that old wives' tale."

Back home I told Joan the news. "I'll have three under three," I said. "I really wasn't expecting that."

Joan was very quiet for a few minutes. "I suppose you'll find a place in your heart for another baby even though unexpected."

Her lukewarm response surprised me, but then I hadn't exactly been overjoyed myself. As this pregnancy advanced, however, I felt something had come between us. Finally, I asked Joan over for coffee so we could talk. At first, she said she was busy, but with a little persuasion agreed to come. When we were settled in the kitchen and the kids were occupied in the front room I asked if I had done something to hurt her.

She stirred her coffee and didn't look up at me. "I'm just having trouble dealing with you being pregnant again," she said. "You already have three healthy children and are happily expecting your fourth." Joan stopped stirring and looked at me. "It just doesn't seem fair."

My heart went out to her. After having a baby boy who was stillborn, she finally gave birth to a daughter, but was told she would never be able to bear more children. Her dreams of a big family were shattered. We had a good, quiet talk that day, but I could tell by her body language she still wanted to keep her distance.

While Chris was at kindergarten that afternoon and the twins were down for a nap, I sat in my favorite chair and began to pray for Joan, our friendship, and the current situation. It was more a prayer of the heart than words, but God heard it and provided a solution. A quiet inner voice said, "Ask Joan to be this baby's godmother."

When John came home from work, I talked to him. He readily agreed. That evening we asked her, and her face lit up with pleasure. "I'd love that," she said. "Thank you."

What a transformation I saw! Instead of staying away, Joan stopped by nearly every day, helping me prepare for the coming baby. Once Nicholas was born, it was as though he had two mothers. With Joan's help, having three under three plus Christopher, now six, was not nearly as difficult as I feared it would be. She was glad to help me shop or to take all the kids to the playground. When my strength was flagging, she would even give me an afternoon of peace and quiet.

One evening at a special church service, I stood next to Joan while the choir sang one of our favorite hymns, "Lord of all hopefulness, Lord of all joy . . .." Joan's face was truly radiant with joy as she held my baby and cuddled him as though he were her own.

Because of her, I had learned something important about prayer. Sometimes God asks us to be part of His answer to a prayer, and when He does, it's a good thing to listen and obey.

Thank You Note

Thank you Holy Father God, for Joan's friendship.
Thank you for my healthy baby.
Thank you for all my children.
Thank you for my wonderful, understanding husband. Thank you
that you love and guide us
and provide our every need.

Hearing Angels

I STILL REMEMBER my first hike with my father, a trek to the top of thirteen-thousand-foot Argentine Pass. "Listen closely," he told me as we ate our lunch. "We're high enough that you just might hear the angels sing."

I said the same to my own children on the many family hikes we made each summer as they were growing up. I have to admit in all the time I have spent high in the Colorado Rockies, I have never actually heard the angels sing. I have, however, had an angel speak to me.

This happened only once, and only because it was, I believe, a life or death message and I simply wasn't hearing it any other way. It happened on a last-of-summer camping trip when the boys were all in their teens.

My husband John and I had chosen a campsite on the shores of a pristine high-country lake situated above ten thousand feet. Aptly named Mirror Lake, its placid, deep waters are home to both Brook and Rainbow Trout, and in the early morning and evening the fishing is good. In between there are plenty of opportunities to hike and explore. Those expeditions were always my favorite activity on our camping trips.

On this particular day, as I prepared lunches for our planned hike to the top of Tincup Pass, I noticed I was uncharacteristically short of breath. In fact, I had been short of breath ever since we pitched our tent the night before. *It must be allergies or a cold coming on,* I told myself. I was born and raised at 8,500 feet above sea level and even though we now lived in Denver, the Mile High city, I had roamed these mountains all my life.

I reasoned that my problem couldn't be the altitude.

On the hike, I lagged farther and farther behind, struggling to breathe. John became concerned and called for a rest stop.

I didn't want to admit to my real problem, so I told him I was having trouble with one of my boots and was afraid I might have a blister. "Go on ahead," I said. "I'll take the boot off and check my foot. I may have to go on back down to camp and doctor it."

Reluctantly, John and our boys left me behind.

I made myself comfortable on a big flat-topped rock by the side of the road and took in the beauty of my surroundings. The weather was perfect—crisp and clear. The sky was a glorious high-altitude blue with just a few wisps of clouds drifting between the formidable bald peaks that flank the pass. High above me, a large hawk was hunting its lunch. It was a weekday and there were no other hikers in sight. No jeeps had been on the road either.

Having caught my breath, I settled back to enjoy the sunshine and scenery before heading back to camp. I reached into my breast pocket and pulled out my cigarettes. I took one out, but as I prepared to light it, I heard a man's voice speaking to me.

"You're going to have to choose, you know."

Startled, I looked all around. There was no one there, yet the voice had sounded like someone was sitting right next to me. I put the cigarette to my lips again. Once more I heard the voice.

"You will have to decide which you love more . . . these mountains or those cigarettes."

There was still no one near, yet the voice sounded so real, so determined. I looked up at the towering peaks above me and thought, *I'm not about to give up these magnificent hills that have been my home all my life.*

I put the cigarettes in my pocket and headed back to camp. That evening after dinner, John started a fire. When it was going good, I took the cigarettes out of my pocket and threw them into the flames. My husband, who had stopped smoking some ten years before, looked surprised. Then I heard a quiet whisper in the depths of my mind. It was the mysterious voice from my aborted hike.

Good choice, He said.

I've always wondered about that voice. Was it God? Was it an angel? Was it the Holy Spirit speaking aloud? I won't know until I walk through the gates of Heaven, but this I do know. God spoke that day to a young mother and changed my life for the better. I suspect that voice came about through someone's prayers for me.

I learned through that experience that someone had been praying for me, and Holy Father God had answered their prayers in a very specific way. Not only can we trust God for the prayers we pray for ourselves, but we can also thrust Him with the prayers we pray for others. There is nothing too big or small for Him.

Thank You Note

Thank you Holy Father God
for speaking to me in a very direct and personal way
when cigarettes threatened my well being.
Thank you for granting me the grace to quit.
Thank you I have never wanted
to take up smoking again.

Holy Spirit
GPS

NOW THAT WE ARE OLDER, my husband lets me do most of the driving. So one bright sunny morning, I pulled out of our driveway and signaled a left turn at the end of the block.

"Why are you turning left?" John asked.

"I thought we'd take the scenic route today," I said with a smile.

"Honey, we'll be late. Take the direct route. We can do your scenic route coming back."

I sighed. The summer morning was too pretty to allow an argument. Even though I had a strong feeling it was a mistake, I turned right instead.

John's direct route was a busy six-lane state highway with traffic signals every few blocks. And when traffic is heavy you can count on stopping at every last one of them. Today's traffic seemed to be moving smoothly enough when we turned onto the highway.

Maybe this isn't a bad choice after all, I thought.

"I don't know how you come up with some of the crazy ways you choose to go places," John said, half teasing, half serious.

As I drove, I thought about a way to explain. I wanted him to know my route selection wasn't quite as random as it might have seemed. When we lived in the city where most streets were laid out on a grid, route finding was simple. However, upon John's retirement, we moved to a suburb that had once been a farming community. Unless the destination was somewhere along the highway, there was seldom a direct route to anywhere. The streets meandered along the channels of three different creeks, and numerous irrigation canals wound their way through neighborhoods. Two railroads also sliced through town adding confusion.

Tired of getting lost, even after looking at a map, I had started praying for directions. To my amazement God answered those prayers, but I wasn't sure how to tell John. While I was mulling over how to explain, the road ahead suddenly filled with brake lights. Traffic slowed to a crawl.

"Probably construction," John said. "Hopefully we can get through it quickly."

Locals have a standing joke that there are only two seasons in Colorado—winter and construction. "Hopefully," I echoed but was doubtful. In a forty-five-miles-per-hour zone, we were barely moving ten.

When we finally reached the crest of a hill, flashing red-and-blue lights from three police cars, two ambulances, and a fire truck made the problem obvious. Several vehicles had been involved in a collision at the bottom.

"I guess we should have taken your scenic route after all," John mumbled.

We were at a virtual standstill while three lanes of traffic on our side of the highway merged into the one-lane police had opened. *This*, I thought, *is my opportunity to explain.*

"When you were a kid did you ever do a penny walk," I asked.

John stared at me. "No. Never," he said. "I have no idea what you are talking about."

"My friends and I used to do a penny walk on long summer days when we were bored. At every intersection you flip a coin. Heads you go straight. Tails you turn."

John nodded, still looking perplexed.

"Then," I continued, "if the result is turn, you flip again. Heads right. Tails left."

"And how often did you get lost?" he asked.

"Never. Just in case, someone kept track of the street names and turns, but we always managed to end up right back where we started."

John threw a hand up in the air. "So, what was the point?"

"Well . . . we got to explore our neighborhood and discover new things we hadn't known were there. One day we came upon a little park with a delightful sunken garden we'd never seen before. Another day, we discovered a little mom-and-pop grocery where we bought some penny candy and sodas out of a tub of ice. It was fun."

"Please don't tell me you flip a coin to decide which way to go when you drive," John said.

"No. But when we moved here, I found myself getting lost far too often. So, I started asking Holy Father God to help me plan my route. Then, when I was uncertain at an intersection, I would ask Him to head me in the right direction. He's never failed me."

"So . . . are you telling me God wanted us to take the scenic route today?"

"Yes. I don't always hear correctly, but more often than not, I do. And when I ignore Holy Father God's instruction, I can end up in messes like this one."

John shook his head. "From now on, instead of second guessing you when we go places together, I'll try to remember to pray *with* you."

I learned that day that God honors a heart that chooses not to argue. My choice of going along with John provided Holy Father God with an opportunity to draw the two of us closer together. After all, two praying is always better than one."

Thank You Note

Thank you Holy Father God
there is no matter too small or trivial
to bring before you.
Thank you we don't need to flip a coin
to decide how to turn.
Thank you that you see beyond what we can see
and your directions are always good.

Murphy's Law

IT WAS A MURPHY'S LAW KIND OF DAY. You know the kind, one of those days when if something can possibly go wrong, it will. I overslept my alarm by an hour. At first, I didn't think that would be such a problem because the only thing we had on our agenda was a wedding rehearsal and dinner in the evening. I dressed quickly, said my morning prayers, and read my daily devotional and scriptures asking God to direct my day.

In the meantime, my presently wheelchair-bound husband had wheeled himself out of the bedroom and was waiting for breakfast.

Most mornings, John likes oatmeal with fruit and nuts. I opened the drawer where I kept the saucepan. Not there. I discovered it in the sink where I had left it the day before. I washed it up and reached for the oats. You guessed it. The canister was empty.

"Would you like scrambled eggs with cheese for a change," I called to John from the kitchen.

"Sure," he said not realizing it was actually the only choice he had this morning.

I put four slices of bread in the toaster and got out four eggs, but then I discovered we were out of cheese. "How about plain scrambled eggs," I called again.

"Whatever." He had probably figured out it was a rhetorical question. A glance at the clock told me it was getting late and this would be more brunch than breakfast. Poor John was probably just hoping for something, anything, to eat.

John was only a few days out of rehab after breaking his leg, and I was having a hard time adjusting my daily activities as his primary caregiver. I planned this to be an easy day, but after getting a late start on breakfast I wasn't so sure.

Early in the afternoon, I helped John clean up and get dressed. Then I took my own shower. We should have had the rest of the afternoon to enjoy each other before our son Dan would return home from work to help me get John and wheelchair into the car and off to the rehearsal. But when I rejoined John in the family room, he had spilled coffee all over himself. I tried hard not to grumble as I helped him change his clothes.

"I need suspenders with these pants, " he said, after I finally had him dressed.

"You're in wheelchair, "I snapped. "Why would you need suspenders? Besides, I don't know where they are." After returning from rehab, our boys had completely redone our bedroom to accommodate John's wheelchair. A dresser had been moved out, and neither John nor I knew where its contents had ended up.

"Where's the printout of the ceremony?" John asked. As a pastor, he would be the one to lead the ceremony from his wheelchair.

"I gave it to you," I said, trying to stay calm.

He shrugged. "It might be on my desk."

I looked on the desk, but of course it wasn't there. After looking several places it wasn't, we finally found it in the container along with all his prescription medicines. By then it was almost time for our son to arrive, but another complication came through the door.

Our twenty-year-old grandson hobbled in. "I think I broke my foot at work," he said. "I need Dad to take me to Urgent Care."

"But," I said, "I'm counting on your dad to take me and Grandpa to the rehearsal and dinner."

"I almost forgot," John called out. "Your brother called while you were in the shower. He needs a call back. He's sick again."

I threw my hands in the air. "Did you tell him the wedding rehearsal is tonight?" My voice had raised more than I meant for it to.

"No," John said. "I just told him you would call later."

By the time Dan finally arrived, he discovered me fussing at his father for being a lousy communicator, his son Ben pleading to be driven to urgent care, and John asking for help getting to the bathroom one more time before we left.

Unflappable, Dan took the situation in hand and told me to call my brother while he took John to the bathroom. He also reassured Ben he would take him to Urgent Care once we were on our way to the rehearsal. He even found a report binder in his desk for the wedding ceremony printout. Everything seemed to be looking up. But as Dan was transferring John from the wheelchair to the car, the importance of suspenders became apparent.

Between wheelchair and car, John's pants fell to his ankles.

There was no time to search for the missing suspenders. We pulled up his pants, sat him in the car, and I jumped in the driver's seat. Dan drove his son to the hospital while I drove John to the rehearsal.

A few blocks from home, John said, "Where is the binder with the ceremony?"

"Don't you have it?" I asked.

"No, Dan had it, but he put it down somewhere when he helped me pull my pants up."

I pulled over to the side of the road and checked the backseat and the trunk where Dan stowed the wheelchair. No report binder with ceremony. I flipped a U and headed back home. Just a few houses away from ours, I spotted the binder in the middle of the street. Dan must have set it on top of the car and had forgotten it. I retrieved the folder and we were on our way again.

My cell rang. "Where are you?" Our about-to-be-married son Chris asked.

"Almost to the highway," I said. "Sorry we're late."

"Well don't get on the highway or you'll be really late. There's an accident, and traffic is backed up for miles."

Chris gave me instructions on how to reach the wedding venue using city streets. I didn't pay a great deal of attention, because I thought I knew exactly where it was, but I was wrong yet again.

I drove right past the entrance to the wedding venue, and spent a frustrating five minutes trying to figure out where it could be. I called Chris. He gave me very specific instructions using landmarks to find the place, and we finally made it. We were only thirty minutes late.

The whole wedding party was standing around waiting for us when we drove up.

"Don't worry about it, Mom," Chris said as he opened the car door to help his dad out. "We still have plenty of time to do the rehearsal and get to dinner."

I tried to warn Chris, but too late. He was already helping his dad up. Down went the pants in front of all those people!

I'm pretty sure the bride gasped, but for the most part people were very polite, hiding their smiles and turning away.

John set his jaw firm while Chris pulled his pants up and sat him in the chair before wheeling him off to the rehearsal.

I was no longer needed and gave a sigh of relief. I found a shady bench and sat down while the others were occupied with the rehearsal. There was a brook splashing into a pond in the garden, and roses were in bloom and scenting the air. A pair of wild geese had taken up residence by the pond. They were shepherding a gaggle of goslings while they grazed in the green grass.

"Where did I go wrong with this day Holy Father God," I quietly prayed. "I started it out right. I even asked for your direction, but then everything went wrong."

I sat still waiting for the answer when it hit me like a ton of bricks. I had planned just such a day, I realized. I had asked for God's direction, but then I had taken it all into my own hands. I hadn't stopped, even for a moment, to ask God why things kept going wrong.

I realized then that asking for God's direction at the beginning of the day, doesn't really mean much unless I also consult Him throughout the day. It's important to turn to God at all times and hear what He has to say.

"Sorry, God," I prayed. "Please help me to seek your direction throughout my days.

Since that time, I try to remember to stop and ask Holy Father God for direction and help whenever I am having a Murphy's law kind of day. Perhaps that's why He allows them in the first place, so we will stop and seek His advice.

Thank You Note

Thank you Holy Father God
that you are always faithful,
even when I am not.
Thank you for leading us to retrace our steps
and find the printout of the wedding ceremony.
Thank you for alerting Chris to tell us to stay off the highway.
Thank you for helping the wedding rehearsal go smoothly
in spite of my many missteps.

No Magic Formula

MY LATE MOTHER-IN-LAW, a lifelong Roman Catholic, had a favorite "magic" formula for finding things. She would enlist the aid of St. Anthony, recite a specified number of Creeds, "Hail Mary's" and "Our Father's," and then simply go on about her business until the lost item turned up. It really bugged me that an intelligent, educated woman like Mom Farrow would resort to such a seemingly old-fashioned, superstitious form of prayer. I was even more bugged that her method nearly always worked—for her, that is. My own luck with it is not so good.

Only last week, I misplaced a terrific greeting card I found for a special friend. Pressed for time, I decided to give Mom Farrow's formula a try. I asked St. Anthony's help and recited the prescribed prayers. Then I started searching. Certain I had left the card on my desk, I shuffled and reshuffled everything on the desktop. While I was shuffling, I noticed a reference book I needed for the article I was currently writing was not where I thought I had left it.

I continued my search for the greeting card while also thinking about the reference book. I looked in drawers, on the file cabinet next to the desk, as well as the bookshelves above it. Then I remembered I had taken the reference book to the bedroom with me the night before to do a bit more reading, so I continued searching for the greeting card, muttering, "Holy Father God, where is it?" while repeatedly looking where it was not.

Finally, I gave up on the card, thinking Mom Farrow's prayer formula did not work. I resolved to make time to shop for another greeting card and returned to my work. Before long, I needed to retrieve the reference book from my bedroom shelf.

Imagine my surprise when I picked up the reference book and the missing greeting card fluttered to the floor. I must have absent mindedly closed it inside that book the evening before.

Suddenly the real reason for the success of Mom Farrow's prayer formula hit me.

The secret wasn't the number or combination of prayers that she prayed, but rather, having prayed them, she could let go and get on with her business while God did the work. I, on the other hand, had been trying to do the work for God.

"I'm sorry Holy Father God," I prayed. "You kept bringing that book to my mind, but I was too busy relying on my own efforts to listen."

I've learned since then to listen more and do less. A formula is just a formula. Just because it works for one person, doesn't mean it will work for everybody. There is no magic quality to prayer. Prayer is simply communication with a Holy Father God who cares.

Thank You Note

Thank you Holy Father God
that it is never necessary to jump through hoops
or make incantations to catch your attention.
Thank you that a simple prayer is all you require.
Thank you for hearing and caring.

When in Doubt, Don't

ONE SPRING, A COUPLE JOINED our church who had two boys, one the age of our oldest, Chris, and one the age of our twins. The boys all met in Sunday school and really got along well. I sought out Jim and Sam's parents in the adult class and introduced myself.

"Nice to meet you," Julie said. "We heard from a neighbor this is a really friendly church." Julie, the wife, said. "Our boys love the Sunday school. They really like your boys too. They've told us all about them."

"Only good things, I hope. Our guys seldom get into serious trouble, but I know they are far from perfect angels."

She laughed. "Boys are boys. Mine are a handful too," she said.

Soon Julie and Tom were active in the church in so many ways it made my head spin. Tom taught a Sunday school class and offered to start a Boy Scout troop. Julie virtually took over the women's group and spurred us into activities we'd never even considered before.

Under Julie's leadership we put on a carnival that summer, complete with a silent auction. Julie, a real estate agent, had made lots of contacts in the business community and was a genius at getting donations. She even managed to acquire a new car for a raffle.

Our boys spent a lot of time together too. Instead of picnics and hikes in the mountains (my idea of summer fun), Julie took her boys to movies and the swimming pool. She often invited my boys to come along, even paying their way at the movies.

John and I also started doing things with Tom and Julie as couples. They had a beautiful home twice the size of ours and the boys loved to play there. Julie would arrange a babysitter for all the kids at her house, and we would go out for dinner or to a show.

Sometimes we entertained Tom and Julie with a barbeque at our house, but I always felt our home was really shabby and our hospitality lacking compared to theirs. So I was surprised one night when Julie called and asked if she and Tom could come over.

After they arrived Julie said, "We have a business proposition for you two." Tom nodded in agreement. Julie looked at him. "Why don't you explain what we have in mind."

"Well," Tom said, "we have a side business flipping houses."

"Flipping houses?" John asked.

"Yes," Julie chimed in. "As a real estate agent, I come across distressed properties. When we buy them, Tom uses his construction experience to make them look great on a shoestring budget. Then we sell at a nice profit."

"But doesn't that take a lot of money up front?" I asked.

"It does. That's why we wanted to talk with you."

Julie explained they had found an ideal property for flipping, but they had recently put all their liquid assets toward purchasing their home.

"I don't see how we can help," John said. "Our budget barely allows for some savings toward the boys' education."

"But you have equity in this house," Julie said. "You've been here what? Ten years? I'll bet it's worth double, maybe even triple, what you paid for it."

"You're suggesting we refinance?" John said. "The house may be worth more, but interest rates are higher right now. It wouldn't make sense."

"No, no," Tom said. "You wouldn't have to do that. Julie will use her financial contacts to arrange a bridge loan backed by the equity in your home. There won't even be any payments until the property sells. Construction companies take out bridge loans all the time."

"I feel sure," Julie said, "God wants you to be a part of this wonderful opportunity. The owner will let John and Tom assume her first mortgage. We use the bridge loan to cover all expenses. John can help Tom with the work on the weekends. Then we sell, pay off the bridge loan, and split the profits."

John and I said it sounded good, but we would like to have an attorney draw up a contract. Both Tom and Julie looked offended. "What for," Tom said. "We're all Christians. We don't need a contract."

"Let's pray about it," Julie said. "The owner is a single mom who really needs to sell. You'll love her," she added, playing on our sympathies.

We held hands around the table and bowed our heads for prayer. Julie led, praising God for the wonderful opportunity and for showing how it could be accomplished. She also prayed for Barbara, the current owner, and her children, asking God to help them find them a safe affordable new place to live.

Julie and Tom's proposition did sound like a win-win for everyone. So in the end we agreed and the next day Julie set the wheels in motion for the bridge loan.

John spent several weekends and a few evenings working with Tom. Julie proved resourceful when it came to acquiring things needed for the remodel. She found practically new kitchen cabinets at a garage sale. She also bought carpeting from an installer at a huge discount. It had been special ordered for a customer who turned it down when it came. I took care of all the kids so the others could work. The remodel went well and was just finished when interest rates went up and the housing market slowed way down.

The due date on the bridge loan was only a few weeks away when I asked Julie if she had any prospective buyers. "Nobody's buying houses in this market," she snapped.

I was taken aback. "Then what about the bridge loan?"

"You and John will have to figure that out," she said. "Tom and I have our own troubles." She was brusque and cranky, not the friendly, easy-going Julie I had come to know.

I told John about it when he came home from work. "Tom has been really edgy too," John said. "They're dependent on Julie's income and her sales have all but dried up."

"I'm worried about the bridge loan," I said.

"Me too. But all we can do right now is pray for a quick sale. I'm afraid there won't be much profit to split in this real estate market."

Together John and I prayed for a quick sale of the remodeled house. We also prayed for Tom and Julie, asking God's provision for them and their children.

A few evenings later, Julie stopped by unannounced and told us she had filed for divorce and their house was in foreclosure. She also told us the house we had helped remodel would soon be in foreclosure if it weren't sold. "The bridge loan money is gone," she said. "You can't expect us to make payments on that mortgage when we can't pay our own," she said.

We were devastated. Why hadn't we insisted on that contract? Sadly, we had been listening more intently to Tom and Julie than to Holy Father God. Now, unless God intervened, we could lose our own home too. There was no way we could make payments on two houses, let alone pay off the bridge loan and purchase their share of the equity.

After Julie left, John and I held hands and prayed. "We're sorry, Holy Father God, that we rushed into this deal without taking time to hear what you had to say. Please show us now how we can come out of this whole."

That night I had a dream. Tornados are rare but not unheard of in the Denver area and, in my dream, I saw a tornado headed straight for our house. John and I just stood there with our children gathered around us paralyzed with fear. When the tornado was practically upon us, it suddenly lifted up and jumped over our house, missing us completely. I woke from the dream feeling reassured God would give us a solution that would let us keep our home.

At breakfast John said, "I'm going to take the afternoon off so we can do what we should have done before we took out that bridge loan."

"What is that?" I asked.

"Talk to our own bank."

We explained the situation to the loan officer. He shook his head. "That bridge loan should never have been granted," he said. "That's not what a bridge loan is for." Then he added that if we had enough equity in our home, and he thought we did, we could do a second mortgage.

The second mortgage would provide enough money to pay the bridge loan and buy Tom and Julie's interest in the property. It would also buy us time. We would, however, be responsible for the payments on both the first mortgage, which John had assumed on the other property, and the second mortgage on our property.

"I don't see how we can manage that," John said, "unless we get a very quick sale at a good price."

The loan officer then suggested something we'd never even thought of. We could rent the property to cover the payments on both the first and second mortgages. "Eventually, when the market improves," he said, "You can sell it and possibly even come out ahead."

That night, after the kids were in bed, John hugged me and said, "I am so relieved to know there's a way out of this mess."

"Me too." Then after a quiet moment I added, "Strange though, I'm more upset we allowed ourselves to be sucked into this deal than I am with Tom and Julie."

John was thoughtful. "It's hard to be angry with people who are in the process of losing everything. Their home, their marriage, all gone."

"And we still have our home and each other," I said.

John smiled. "Tom and Julie used us, but God is faithful. I think he was trying to tell us to go slow the night they came over with their wonderful deal. We just weren't listening."

"I think you're right," I said. "I know I had doubts, but Julie kept overriding them."

I curled up against John and he put his arm around me. "Let's make a promise to each other and to God," he said. "In the future, whenever someone says God wants us to do something, let's always say we will—as soon as God also tells us."

In the end we were able to keep our home, but only by the grace of God and through much prayer.

I learned from that experience that it is always better to consult Holy Father God and pay attention to His quiet promptings, no matter how well-meaning a friend might be. Only God knows the future, and He's the only one who knows what's best for us.

Thank You Note

Thank you Holy Father God
for saving our home.
Thank you for strengthening our marriage
through this experience when it could have torn it apart.
Thank you for teaching us to pay attention
when another person claims
to have a word from you for us
and we feel a check in our spirits.

Part Four

Running on Empty?
Recharge!

There comes a time
to turn off the music, close the book,
and just be with God

God on the Mountain

WHEN I WAS A YOUNG GIRL, I loved spending time in Grandma's kitchen. On this particular day, her kitchen was still fragrant with the warm aroma of bread she had baked early that morning. I cut two thick slices from one of the now cooled loaves and made a sandwich with peanut butter and homemade raspberry jam.

"I thought I'd take a hike," I said as I tucked my sandwich in a baggy and put it in my daypack. I was in sixth grade, but Grandma trusted me to take familiar hikes by myself.

Grandma turned from the sink where she had been washing up and wiped her hands on her apron. "Have you finished your chores?"

"Yes ma'am. I swept the porch. Then I deadheaded the pansies, cut a big bouquet of sweet peas for the front room and watered the petunias in the porch boxes."

Grandma nodded. "Then okay. Where are you planning to go?"

I added an apple and a Coke to my pack along with the Nancy Drew mystery I was reading. "I thought I'd take the trail to Highland Park," I said.

I saw Grandma's eyebrows start to rise.

"Not all the way," I quickly added. "Just to that meadow below the first mine dump, not clear up to Grandpa Rubado's mine. There's a big flat rock where I like to eat my lunch and read."

"Well, don't be gone too long. You don't want to be out when the storms start rolling off the peaks this afternoon."

I had walked every trail accessible from our mountain home with my parents and grandparents and knew them all like the back of my hand. My folks trusted me to go out on short hikes by myself as long as I told them where I was going and made sure to return by midafternoon. Our summer days started out bright and sunny, but typically thunderheads would form later on, bringing lightning, wind and rain to our mountain valley.

I started up the trail which zigzagged through dense spruce forest. It was always hard work going up the trail, especially wearing the shirt jacket Grandma always made me wear just in case the weather changed. Halfway up I stopped to remove the shirt and tie it around my waist.

When I looked up, a chipmunk was sitting on the side of the trail staring at me. He looked so cute and wasn't bothered at all by me staring back at him. His cheeks were fat with seeds from the cone he held in his front paws. I watched him until he skittered off into the woods.

This kind of encounter was why I endured the long hike up the mountain. Watching animals was one of my favorite things. There were no scary animals in our woods like mountain lions or wolves, but there was always something fun to see.

I headed out again, and before long reached my destination, a little grassy meadow ringed with aspen trees. I spread my shirt out like a tablecloth on my favorite rock and set out my lunch. Then I took out my Nancy Drew mystery and read while I ate.

I was cozy and warm siting in the sunshine and completely absorbed in the adventures of Nancy Drew when something caused me to suddenly look up. I hadn't heard a noise. No one had called my name. But it was as if something had called my attention. Something I couldn't identity.

I looked around me. There seemed to be a change in the atmosphere. The light looked different than before. The air was so very still and quiet. Not even a breeze. And then, to my amazement, a small herd of deer entered the meadow. I sat very still while they all moved out into the open and grazed in the warm grass around me.

Joy bubbled up in my heart. Even at that young age I knew I had witnessed something special. Something otherworldly. It wasn't frightening. In fact, I felt no fear at all. I kept still, savoring the special moment. It wasn't until I noticed by the low position of the sun that I realized it was past time for me to start home.

I slid the apple core in my empty sandwich bag and stuffed it, the empty Coke can, and book into my pack. Gathering up my shirt, I slid off the rock as quietly as possible, hoping to not disturb the deer. But my feet no sooner touched the ground than the deer melted into the trees. It was almost as if they had never been there in the first place.

The clearing remained peaceful but now felt empty. Yet I knew a presence beyond myself had been there only moments before.

I hurried down the trail, knowing I was late and not wanting to worry Grandma, but also knowing I had experienced something amazing. It was the first time I had felt the near presence of God, though I wouldn't fully understand that until much later.

I have never experienced a time when I did not believe in God, though I often hear others talk of their conversion experiences. But that day in the meadow, when I felt the near presence of Holy Father God, changed things for me.

To this day, I understand the importance of taking time to be alone with God in the beauty of His creation, There is so much evil going on in the world, but you can always find the beauty of God in His creation. And it's one of the places where I can best hear His voice.

Thank You Note

Thank you Holy Father God
that you are everywhere present
in your creation.
Thank you for the beauty of your creatures—
deer, chipmunks, butterflies,
flowers and trees—
all the work of your hand!
Thank you for creating this beautiful world
and sharing it with me.

Father
Knows Best

WHEN I WAS A CONTRACT WORKER in the word processing and publications department of a large communications company, a co-worker introduced me to the prosperity gospel and "name-it-and-claim-it" prayer. It began when she came in uncharacteristically late and very upset one morning.

"My car burned up on the highway this morning," she said with tears in her eyes. "I only have the minimum insurance on that old car, so I don't know how I'll replace it."

Lois was a single mom whose ex-husband had run up so many bills she had to claim bankruptcy after their divorce to get out from under the burden. After calming down a bit, she called a friend from her church for prayer and advice. She was smiling at the end of the conversation. "I just needed to be reminded my God will supply all my needs according to His riches in glory," she said paraphrasing Philippians 4:19. "I'm laying claim to a new car."

And indeed, the next day she drove to work in a brand-new red Toyota Corolla. Her insurance agent had told her about a dealership that had a second chance program for people in just her situation. I was impressed with this different kind of prayer. So, when a position in our department came open for hiring, I asked her to show me how to pray for it.

"You and your husband are faithful church goers and givers. We'll just claim the job as yours," Lois said. Then she cited Malachi 3:10 (NRSV), "Bring the full tithe into the storehouse, so that there may be food in my house, and thus put me to the test, says the Lord of hosts; see if I will not open the windows of heaven for you and pour down for you an overflowing blessing."

I applied for the job and Lois put in a good word with the department head for me. She also gave me a beautiful greeting card congratulating me on my new position to "seal the deal," so to speak.

I waited expectantly for my interview, but days went by without word.

Then lightning struck. The management of the company had a budget meeting. In a cost-cutting measure, they not only eliminated the job I had applied for, but they eliminated the entire department. Suddenly, I was without a job at all.

I thought my faith had grown to the point where it could withstand anything, but this blow sent me reeling. Lois got her car when she needed it. I needed this job. Why was it taken from me?

Not long after losing my job, a small software developer ran an ad in our local paper for an administrative assistant/technical writer. The job description fit my qualifications perfectly. I sent my resumé and within a few days the owner called me for an interview. My heart soared as I entered Gene Goldhammer's office, but it fell when I saw the stack of resumés on his desk. I was sure any one of those resumés had more experience and better qualifications than I did.

"Do you have any experience with a relational database?" Gene asked. "My software is a complex database that tracks inventory, ordering and sales, but if you're familiar with any modern database you can probably pick it up quickly."

I shifted in my chair. I was pretty sure I didn't have the knowledge he was looking for. "My database experience is limited," I said, "but I do have basic familiarity."

"Good enough," he said to my surprise. "The user manual is written in Word, and I see you're very experienced with that. Have you ever put together a training manual?"

"I wrote a manual to teach Word to Word Perfect users at my last job," I said. "I also helped put together a training manual for employees who would be working outside the United States."

Gene tipped the entire stack of resumés on his desk into his waste basket. "When can you start?" he asked.

"M-Monday," I stammered in amazement.

I soon learned that working for Gene was a far better situation than the job I had so coveted with the large communications company. Not only was he one of the kindest, most understanding men I've ever worked for, the work itself was varied, challenging, and immensely satisfying. The pay was also as much as I had been making. Moreover, my hours were flexible, a real blessing for a mom with four teenage boys and an even greater blessing when I needed to take time off to help my mother with her battle with non-Hodgkin's lymphoma.

When Mother's oncologist said he had run out of treatment options and transferred her to home hospice care, I tried my best to give her the help she needed. She lived in a neighboring city about a forty-minute drive from work, and every day I would leave work as early as possible to make the trip to assist her. As she grew weaker, I stayed with her long into the evening, often not getting home until bedtime.

Gene noticed that I was becoming more and more exhausted when I came into work. One day he called me into his office.

"Sarah," he said, "your mother needs you far more than I do right now. Don't worry about your job. I'll make do with temps and keep it open for you. Take as much time as you need to be with your mother until the end."

I was overwhelmed to tears by his generosity. I could hardly believe what he was saying. The big communications company I had wanted to work for would never have made me an offer like that. I took Gene at his word, thanking my Holy Father God for a boss who understood both the importance of family and my need to be with my mother in her last weeks on earth.

Looking back, I now understand the reason why Lois received her reliable new car and I did not receive the job I claimed. "Name-it-and-claim-it" prayer limits God to a specific answer, but God being God will often give us something better instead of giving in to our way.

Lois' request was reasonable and necessary, so she got the car. My request was not within Father God's will for me. He had something *better* in mind.

Now I try to keep my mind open. Instead of naming and claiming something specific I lift up my petition to God and wait for His answer. Often His answer is one that would have never occurred to me and His answer is *always* the best.

Thank You Note

Thank you Holy Father God
that you know my needs
often before even I know them.
Thank you that your answers to my prayers
are often so much better than the answers I seek.
Thank you for your faithfulness
to care for me and my family
in each and every
circumstance.

Jesus at the Wheel

WHENEVER I HEAR CARRIE UNDERWOOD sing her song about Jesus taking the wheel, I remember the day in March many years ago when Jesus was at the wheel of our old VW Bug as I drove seventy miles through heavy snow with a friend's fourteen-year-old daughter in the passenger seat.

My friend Sue had invited me to join her for a private retreat at Mt. St. Francis, a convent and retreat center nestled against the foothills west of Colorado Springs. She planned to leave Thursday morning. I didn't want to leave until after school on Friday.

"Great," she said. "That solves a problem for me. Debbie wants to come too, but I don't want to take her out of school."

As John left for work Friday morning, he cautioned me to keep an eye on the weather. "Leave as early as possible. There's a storm coming in," he said, "but it's not expected to reach us until tonight."

The morning was crisp and bright when I went to the grocery store to stock up for John and the boys over the weekend. The sun was still shining and there was no hint of trouble later that day when I filled the tank with gas. In Colorado we joke that if you don't like the weather, wait a minute. But I wasn't worried. I was sure God would accommodate our desire to spend time with Him in retreat.

By the time I picked up Debbie, clouds had rolled in and there were a few flakes of fine, light snow in the air. I still wasn't concerned. I had the car radio on and the forecast for the Denver area predicted less than half an inch of snow.

Debbie settled into the passenger seat. "Would you mind turning the radio off, Mrs. Farrow?" She asked. "I have a book with me I need to finish so I can write a book report when I get home Sunday."

I obliged. Wind noise at high speeds made it hard to listen to the radio anyway. Debbie opened her book and started to read. I got on the highway and headed toward the Springs.

South of Denver the snow was heavier, but nothing our sure-footed Bug with snow tires couldn't handle easily. Icy patches had already been sanded. Traffic was a bit slower than usual but moving right along. Sue had told me dinner at the convent was served at 5:30. Since we were on the road by 3:30 I figured we would be there in plenty of time.

Really heavy snow was coming down when we came into Castle Rock. Debbie asked if we could stop and get something to drink, but I told her I thought we had better stay on the highway and not waste any time. So, she went back to her reading.

Now I was becoming worried. There are few services between Castle Rock and Monument. Between them is Monument Hill, which is notoriously dangerous mountain pass in a storm.

At the southern edge of Castle Rock, the highway patrol closes a gate when storms make driving treacherous. I was relieved to see the gate was open, thinking the highway must not be in bad shape.

I was only a few hundred yards down the road when I saw a patrol car with flashing lights in my rearview mirror. I watched as it pulled up to the gate and the patrolman closed it. Only then did I notice there was hardly any traffic coming from the Springs on the other side of the highway.

Lord have mercy! I thought. *The gate at Monument must already be closed.*

Debbie was still absorbed in her book, and I didn't want to frighten her, but I was genuinely worried. The wind was whipping snow directly into my windshield and I could only see a few yards ahead. On top of that the lane markers were invisible. The possibility of ice under the snow scared me.

Pulling off on the shoulder seemed a poor idea since I didn't have a cell phone to call for help. And while there was a blanket in the back for warmth if we ran out of gas, I hadn't packed food or water. I reasoned being stranded on the highway could be as dangerous as going on. I slowed to a crawl and prayed.

"Holy Father God," I prayed quietly. "I know you have given complete authority over the natural world to your beloved son, my Lord and Savior, Jesus. Please send Him into this storm to get us safely to Colorado Springs."

The wind outside continued to howl, but I suddenly felt an awesome sense of peace far beyond my understanding. There was a presence inside the car bigger and wiser than me. I looked over at Debbie, wondering if she felt it too. Her book was still open on her lap, but she had nodded off to sleep.

In that space of calm, I began to understand what to do. I remembered John telling me to only use my low beams when visibility is poor. I switched from high beam and immediately could see a little better. The red taillights of two other cars were visible down the road. I also remembered John telling me I could use the lights of other cars to see further in fog or heavy snow. I cautiously sped up a little until I was a safe distance behind them. Sure enough, their lights helped me stay on the road.

After several miles, those cars turned off on a county road. But before I could become concerned, I spotted a semi-truck and trailer not far ahead. I followed the truck until he turned into a truck chain station at the base of Monument Hill. I took a deep breath and continued on. It was almost like I was driving on autopilot, yet at the same time, I had never felt so alert, so assured. I knew my Lord was there in the car with me, an unseen presence lending direction, courage and strength.

The storm was just beginning to let up when I started up Monument Hill. A snowplow was clearing and sanding the road ahead of me. *Thank you, dear Jesus!* I thought. Following the plow, I made it over Monument Hill. On the other side there was still some snow coming down, but nothing like I had experienced coming out of Castle Rock.

Debbie yawned and stretched. "Are we almost there?"

"It's not far now."

"Wow, it's getting dark," she said. "I hope we didn't miss dinner. I thought we'd get there sooner."

"Me too," I said. "You slept through the storm, but I see our exit just ahead."

I turned off and headed toward the convent. Jesus had not dismissed the storm because Colorado farmers depend on heavy spring snows to fill reservoirs so they have water for their crops during the hot, dry summer. Instead, He had indeed taken the wheel and got us to Mt. St. Francis safely.

I still felt strangely calm and at peace. I had started out this trip expecting an encounter with God in the stillness of the convent chapel. Instead, I had an encounter with Him in the midst of a raging storm.

That experience taught me that even though Holy Father God appreciates us taking time away to get alone with Him, He is also in all our moments and empty spaces if we will but look for Him.

Thank You Note

Thank you Holy Father God
that you are the God of the storms
as well as the God of the sunshine.
Thank you for sending
a sure and guiding hand
to lead me through that blizzard to safety.
Thank you for the many times
you have helped me get through
the storms of my life.

Masada

THIS TRIP TO ISRAEL had not turned out the way I expected. Sponsored by a Christian women's organization, I thought it would be like a pilgrimage with opportunities to linger and pray in holy places. I hoped to grow closer to Jesus by seeking Him in prayer in the actual places where He taught and ministered during His time on Earth. Instead, I felt hustled and hurried from place to place, a tourist rather than a pilgrim.

I was excited during our visit to the Western Wall, all that remains of the temple, because I was carrying several of the written prayers of my friends back home. I had promised to tuck them into the cracks of the Wall as is the custom. But our visit coincided with a major Jewish feast, and the enormous crowd gathered there distracted me from prayer.

We spent a marvelous hour one morning on the Sea of Galilee. A group of musicians traveling with us began to sing the song about these being the days of Elijah. Soon everyone, even our Jewish guide, joined in, joyously singing and dancing on the boat. This is a scene I will never forget.

Then there was the picturesque old Arab, with his weathered face and long Bedouin robes, who met us when we disembarked from our bus at the top of The Mount of Olives. He pointed to his saddled donkey and announced he was Jesus' Taxi Service. His grin was so expansive and charming that even our guard, who quickly shooed other Arab street merchants away, let him stay. In exchange for American dollars, a few of us rode the donkey part way as we walked down the twisting, narrow path to the church called *Dominus Flevit,* which means Jesus Wept.

Dominus Flevit is a place I was sure I would be allowed to pray. But it was not to happen. After perhaps five minutes inside we were shooed away. This was a deep disappointment to me as it seemed that most people missed how truly holy was the place where we were standing.

Holiest of all was our visit to the Upper Room where Jesus' followers awaited the coming of the Holy Spirit. There someone spontaneously began to sing in the Spirit with a firm, clear voice. Others joined in and the room filled with glorious, celestial music. I could have stayed there forever, but our experience again was cut short. We had to leave because another group was waiting to enter.

I found the trip exhausting. We visited no less than three holy sites every day. One of the last was a trip to Masada. I was hoping to experience history there because I'm a history buff. It's a wonder when you consider that Herod the Great built two palaces there on a high mesa and devised a method of capturing and storing rainwater so the citadel could be self-sustaining. He even had a bathing pool. I was looking forward to viewing all these special spots and imagining what the people who had lived there had experienced.

I chose the cable car over walking to the top, because when I awakened that morning my foot was painful and swollen. When I looked out of the cable car near the gate, I could see the entire Judean countryside stretched out before me. A desolate land of desert and the Dead Sea. I also looked down on groups of hikers making their way up the narrow "snake path," a one-thousand-three-hundred-foot climb from the floor of the Judean desert to the main gate of Masada. Watching them, I was grateful for the cable car.

"Will there be places along the tour where I can sit?" I asked Naomi, our guide.

"No," she answered. "Why?"

I explained about my foot. "Perhaps I can start out with our group, and if the walking is too much, I can go back to the gate."

She shook her head. "That's not allowed. Once the group leaves the gateway it has to stay together throughout the tour."

I bit my lip, not sure what to do.

Naomi looked at my sandal-clad foot and saw it was indeed swollen. "There is a gift shop and places to sit within the double casemate wall that Herod the Great built to fortify the city," Naomi said gently. "It will be cooler and more comfortable there than out in the ruins. Also, you can watch the video of the site which plays on a continuous loop."

I watched as my group set out to explore the sun-bleached ruins. With a sigh, I settled on a bench set into the wall opposite the video screen. I wasn't really interested in the video. I was tired and disappointed.

This entire trip had created memories I was sure would stay with me, and I was grateful for them. But I felt I would return knowing my Lord no better than I had when I left home.

Then, as I sat there, a question came up deep in my spirit. *What is it that makes a place holy?*

I knew the question came from my Holy Father God. I answered in my mind, *It's the presence of the Lord Jesus.*

"Which is better then? Present in the past or present now?"

"Present now, of course," I quickly answered.

"And where is the Lord present now?"

Suddenly understanding dawned like the light of day. The Lord is present now in His people, the Body of Christ.

It's not location that makes a place holy. It's the people gathered there. During this entire trip I had been looking for the Lord in the past, and that's a good way to learn about Him, but one also comes to know Him through fellowship with His people. And here I was, sitting on the top of Masada having a conversation with my Holy Father God. It made me think of the lines from an old prayer. "Heavenly King, Comforter, Spirit of Truth. You are everywhere present and fill all things . . .."

By the time our group returned from its tour of the ruins of Masada, I rejoined them with a new appreciation for the living presence of our Lord Jesus they represented. This was our last day together, but I knew I would remember our time of fellowship for the rest of my life. And, yes, I would return home knowing my Lord better than when I had left, because He is always with me wherever I go.

Thank You Note

Thank you Holy Father God
that you are with me wherever I go.
Thank you that the living
presence of our Lord Jesus
is manifest in all your people.
Thank you that wherever your people
gather in your name
they stand on Holy Ground.

This is
Church

I GREW UP HIGH CHURCH Episcopalian. That meant I wore a hat, or a little doily called a chapel cap, when I went to church. It also meant vases of flowers and glowing candles. The silver altar vessels were polished until they gleamed. Crisp white linens dressed the altar, and a beautiful embroidered silk brocade frontal matched the elegant vestments of the priest and deacons. Hymns and Gregorian chants floated out from the choir loft above the congregation.

For me as a child, this was church. This is where I learned and grew in my faith and where I first experienced God in formal prayer.

I was thinking about these memories last Christmas while we celebrated Holy Communion in the lunchroom of a locked memory care facility. We had remembered the spiritual needs of a frequently forgotten population, and they expressed their gratitude with tears and voices barely more than a whisper. There was no choir, no organ at our Christmas morning service. No flickering candles nor banks of poinsettias. The altar was a humble table.

The congregation shuffled in with walkers or were pushed in wheelchairs. There were also some wanderers who meandered in and out. One member of our congregation was still able to read. He wore a rosary around his neck and eagerly served as an altar boy. Some others remembered how to make the sign of the cross. A few even remembered responses.

Father John spread a cloth and set out the Holy Bible, his chalice and paten. The candle he lit was battery operated from the dollar store. While he prepared the altar, his congregation chattered and fidgeted. But the moment he said, "In the name of the Father . . .." they became quiet and attentive.

In poverty not unlike Bethlehem's stable Christ was born in that unlikely place.

This too is church.

Father John, like every Orthodox priest and many Catholic and Episcopal priests, has a special cloth with a picture of Jesus descending the cross, the four evangelists, and Bible verses relating to Holy Communion. It's about the size of a table placemat and was blessed by his bishop. Whatever surface he spreads that cloth upon becomes an altar holy to God.

Altars may be as varied as the hood of a jeep in the battlefield, the picnic table in a forest service campground or a tray table in a hospital room. The believers who gather at the altar, be they many or few, are church.

The devotion of our nursing home congregation humbles me. Bodies withered, minds fading away, they still possess a deep-down longing for Christ.

At the end of our Christmas service I sang Silent Night acapella. A dear old soul took my hand and joined in. The next week she didn't remember my name or why I was there. Yet that day, she remembered every single word, and every single note of each verse of that hymn and sang it from her heart.

I've learned from these experiences that Christ meets us in joy and sorrow, in health or pain. The traditional marriage vows mirror his love for us. He takes us for better, for worse, for richer, for poorer, in sickness and in health. Not even death can part us from His love.

But here's the wonder of it all. Christ meets us, His church, wherever two or more are gathered in His name. If we seek Him, Holy Father God meets each of us exactly where we are. The setting and circumstances are immaterial.

Thank You Note

Thank you Holy Father God
that church is more than a building,
more than a worship service,
more than Bible studies,
programs and outreaches.
Thank you that church
is wherever your people
gather in your name.
Thank you that you meet each one of us
in the present moment in our lives.

Messy Altars

I DESPERATELY NEEDED to find more time for God in my life. I regularly attended church on Sunday and a Friday prayer group with my husband, but my personal prayer life was sadly lacking. I was a mother of four growing boys, and keeping up with school activities, sports and household responsibilities filled every minute of my life. Often, the only time I had to read the Bible and pray was before bed, and by then I was too tired to really seek the Lord in prayer. So, when Brother Martin, a Benedictine monk, offered a one-day retreat on prayer, I signed up.

I showed up with a few dozen others to hear Brother Martin's words of wisdom.

"Treat every flat surface before you as an altar," Brother Martin said, "and make whatever you are doing on that surface an offering to Almighty God."

His words resonated with me. It seemed a good thing to make whatever I was doing an offering to God. When he finished his talk, he instructed us to spend time alone quietly before the Lord. We could take a walk outside if we wished, find a spot in the church library or parish hall, or simply stay where we were in one of the pews. The only rule was no talking.

I found a bench next to a flowerbed on the church grounds and sat in the sunshine. What Brother Martin had said about altars made sense to me. One of my greatest pleasures in life was playing the piano. *That's my altar*, I thought, *and I can make a conscious offering of the music I play to God.* I resolved to make time every day to spend at least half an hour at the piano. This would enrich my prayer life and also feed my soul.

Later in the day, Brother Martin made himself available to anyone who wanted his counsel. When my turn came, I eagerly told him about my piano altar and how much I appreciated his teaching.

He smiled. "I'm sure your piano is a beautiful, well-polished altar, and I'm sure your music is a fine offering." He paused and looked straight into my eyes. "Remember, though, I said every flat surface. What other altars do you have in your home?"

I sat back puzzled. Then understanding dawned. "You mean like my ironing board? Or the kitchen counter?"

Brother Martin nodded. "Or even the baby's changing table. Some altars and offerings can be very messy. But our gracious Lord accepts them all."

What an interesting idea, I thought. *I'll have to try it out.*

Back home I became conscious of all the altars in my life. When I made the bed, I offered up the work in thanksgiving for my marriage and prayed for my husband's day at work. Folding laundry on the kitchen table became an offering for my children. I prayed the Lord would keep each of them safe in His tender, loving care.

One of the messiest altars in my home was my desk. It was piled with periodicals, writers' guidelines and rejection notices from my attempts at supplementing our income as a freelance writer. Somehow the end of the money always came before the end of the month.

This altar made me feel both rejected and overwhelmed. I had already sent out half a dozen or so stories to publications and all I had received were rejections. I decided I should pray about taking a part-time job outside the home even though I loved writing. It just didn't seem to be working.

It was with these thoughts I tackled a truly messy altar, my kitchen floor. Our four kids routinely managed to dribble crumbs and spill milk. I swept regularly, but once a week I found it necessary to pull on rubber gloves, fill a bucket with hot soapy water, and grab an old-fashioned scrub brush. As I scrubbed, I talked to the Lord about our family finances and asked for clarity about how to fix them.

I had no sooner dropped down on my hands and knees to do the job than the phone rang. I stripped off a glove and reached up to grab the phone. I was still sitting on the floor. "Hello," I said in a tone of voice designed to let a friend know she should call back later and a salesman know I wasn't buying.

A very polite voice on the other end said, "May I please speak to Sarah."

Something told me I should be equally polite. "This is Sarah," I said sweetly.

"This is Mike Aquilina, the editor of *New Covenant Magazine*. I have the article you wrote for our monthly 'How I Pray Now' feature, and I like it very much."

I couldn't say a word. *He liked my story! Did that mean he was buying it?*

He continued. "I need it cut by about 200 words to fit in the space. Would you like to cut it yourself, or do you want me to cut it?"

For a moment, I couldn't find any words. Then I finally managed to get out. "I'll cut it. When do you need it?"

"By the end of the week if you are able."

I agreed, and after our conversation, I sat down on the wet floor and almost cried. My first sale! And it came just as I was making a work offering from a sticky floor-altar. I didn't need to go outside the home to find work. God gave me work right where I was at and doing something I loved. Mike Aquilina ended up being the first of many editors who loved my stories, and I continue writing to this day.

Brother Martin was right. He had told us that making every flat surface an altar was the most important teaching on prayer he had ever received. I was beginning to see the truth in that.

By making every flat surface an altar, I discovered that I was praying throughout the day. It was like praying without ceasing that the bible talks about. I didn't even have to work at it. Since that time, it has become as natural as breathing to me. My thoughts turn to God all the time.

Thank You Note

Thank you Holy Father God
that you accept messy offerings
from messy altars.
Thank you that you don't expect perfection,
but just a willingness
to offer up our lives to you day by day.
Thank you that you multiply our offerings
back to us in wonderful
and often unexpected ways.

Imagine Good

I LIKED TO WHILE AWAY the forty-minute bus ride to work by reading. This morning I had a new mystery by a favorite author I was looking forward to. I had no sooner opened the book and started to read when I heard, "You wouldn't catch me reading that trash."

Startled, I looked up and saw a woman seated next to me. She was wearing a long black skirt and sensible shoes, and her brown hair was pulled back in a tight bun. She wore no makeup and was glaring at me.

She pointed to the book in my lap.

I didn't know what to say. The book I had been reading was written by a Christian author. Why would anyone think it was trash?

"Fiction," the woman said sharply. "That stuff comes from the evil imagination of man. Read your Bible."

I didn't want to spend my ride in fruitless debate, so I merely shrugged and said, "Yes, ma'am, I shall." Then I went back to reading the mystery.

I heard a loud "harrumph" next to me. Thankfully the woman got off two stops later.

Off and on that morning at work, I pondered where in the New Testament man's imagination is branded as evil. The only passage I could come up with was, "the proud are scattered in the imagination of their hearts," but that says more about pride than it does about imagination.

I was still thinking about imagination at lunch. On nice days, I usually walked to a little park tucked between the office buildings to eat my sandwich and read. I settled on a bench in the shade of a spreading maple and closed my eyes. Then I took my question to the Lord in prayer.

As I did, my imagination took over and the maple became a grove of aspen and spruce rimming a lush, green mountain meadow. A riotous bloom of wildflowers spilled out across the grass. The chatter of other workers enjoying their lunch hours became birdsong and the hum of traffic on the street morphed into the buzz of bees.

Wearing hiking boots and jeans instead of my skirt suit and heels, I sat on a sun warmed rock overlooking a pristine high-country lake. My heart filled with peace.

I know this place is a construct of my imagination compiled from memories of many beautiful wilderness places I have been, but it's my own special prayer place. Even when my world is falling apart around me, I can still come here to pray.

"Is it wrong for me to come here, Lord?" I asked.

"Have you caught the irony of coming to an imaginary place to ask me if it's okay to use your imagination in prayer?"

I looked up to see Jesus sitting next to me as He sometimes does here.

168

This Jesus has dancing dark eyes and a warm smile. Like me, He's wearing hiking boots and jeans. He looked at me kindly and said, "Is it wrong to seek a place of peace and quiet?"

"Sometimes it's necessary, Lord."

"Indeed, it is," Jesus replied. "I often find it so too." He paused to take in the beauty of His creation— the tall mountains, rippling water, sweet scented flowers and warm sun.

"The imagination, Sarah, is a gift. Like any gift, you can use it for good or you can use it for evil. The choice is yours."

"How can I know I've made a good choice?"

"When you aren't sure of your choice, examine the fruit. Peace, for example, is always the fruit of good."

I looked out over the meadow still feeling a bit perplexed. "If this place is a construct of my imagination, how do I know I didn't imagine you to say what I wanted to hear?"

I looked back where He had been sitting, but Jesus had gone. I tried with all my might to imagine Him back, but He would not come. This Jesus may be a construct of my own imagination, but He comes and goes of His own volition, not mine.

"A penny for your thoughts," Judy, a coworker said.

I opened my eyes and realized I was back on the park bench. I felt like I had been gone for hours, but in reality, it was only a few minutes.

"I was just thinking about something a woman said to me on the bus this morning," I said, scooting over for her to sit down. We both took out our sandwiches.

"She must have said something pretty profound," Judy remarked. "You were really lost in thought when I came by."

I nodded. "She told me she never reads fiction," I said, "because it comes from the imagination, and the imagination of man is evil."

"What a sad, drab world she must live in. No imagination! That would mean no music, no art, no theater . . ."

I picked up the recitation. "No fiction, no fashion, no jewelry. There wouldn't even be houses or automobiles. Those all existed first in the architect's or engineer's imagination."

We sat companionably for a while eating our lunches and chatting about projects we were working on. We both realized our own jobs actually depended upon our imaginations.

"I think the imagination is a gift," Judy said. "In fact, you might say, I can't imagine a world without it."

We both laughed as we gathered our things to return to work.

I learned from that experience that it is okay to retreat into my imagination for prayer, because sometimes that's the only peaceful place I can find. And Jesus wants us to meet Him wherever we are.

Thank You Note

Thank you Holy Father God
for the gift of imagination.
Thank you for stories, paintings,
music and theater.
Thank you for all the wonderful fruits
that come from the imaginations
of your people.
Thank you also for the ability
to retreat into our imaginations
to find a moment of quiet and peace.

Visit

www.needlerockpress.com
for future books!

www.Sarahelizabethfarrow.com
for Sarah's blog and updates

Reviews are like gold to authors.

If you have enjoyed this book,

please consider leaving a review

on Amazon

Goodreads

or

share on your

favorite social media.

SARAH ELIZABETH FARROW
Sarah Elizabeth Farrow's prayer journey began in childhood while she sat alongside her mother and prayed for her father who was fighting in the "Big War." Her journey has taken many twists and turns, and even a few sidetracks since then, but prayer has guided her throughout her life. She began her writing career fresh out of  school. First, she wrote fashion copy for a large department store, and later graduated to writing and producing radio and television commercials for an advertising agency.

While staying home to raise her four children, Sarah supplemented the household income by writing for a wide range of magazines and newspapers. Sarah now prays and writes from Arvada, Colorado where she lives with John, her husband of 53 years.

Sarah loves hearing from her readers.
You can reach her at
sefarrow43@gmail.com

CPSIA information can be obtained
at www.ICGtesting.com
Printed in the USA
LVHW111329221219
641387LV00001B/79/P